TOWN AND CITY MAPS
OF THE BRITISH ISLES
1800–1855

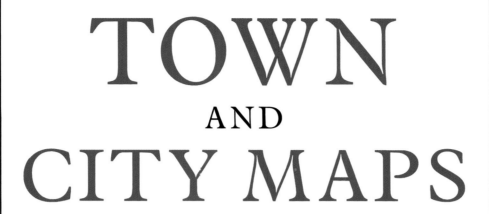

TOWN
AND
CITY MAPS
OF THE BRITISH ISLES
1800-1855

ASHLEY BAYNTON-WILLIAMS

STUDIO EDITIONS

LONDON

PUBLISHER'S NOTE

The majority of cities and towns represented in this volume are
English with comparatively few plans from Ireland, Scotland
and Wales. This uneven distribution is representative of the
cartographic trends of the period and is in no way indicative of
any prejudice on the part of the publishers. The facts and
figures that appear in the captions have been taken from various
different sources (see Bibliography) and in general they refer to
the date of publication of the map. Dates for population figures
have been given wherever these were available.

This edition published by Studio Editions Ltd,
Princess House, 50 Eastcastle Street,
London, W1N 7AP, England.
Copyright © Studio Editions Ltd, 1992
Text copyright © Ashley-Baynton Williams, 1992

Printed and bound in Spain

ISBN 1 85170 941 X

Contents

Town plans of the British Isles

The last eighty years have seen heightened interest in the early mapping of the British Isles, both among museums and among private collectors; this interest, however, has been largely confined to the maps of the individual counties. Town plans, often issued by the same publishers as the county series, compared favourably both in terms of their design and execution, but have not attracted the same attention. This is surprising, particularly as the town plans provide such important indications of the great social revolution that occurred during the nineteenth century, as urbanization dramatically increased in pace.

This great transformation, which had such effect on the face of so many towns of the British Isles, arose out of the Industrial Revolution of the late eighteenth and early nineteenth centuries. While the roots of the Industrial Revolution lie in the eighteenth century, it was the first half of the nineteenth century that saw the scientific discoveries transformed into tangible realities, as understanding turned into application. Perhaps the single greatest catalyst of change was James Watt's invention of the steam-engine, harnessing power for practical use. This discovery not only made possible the factory economy but also led to the introduction and widespread development of the railway network, which linked the factories together, and then provided the means of moving factory products to distribution centres and ultimately to their markets, whether in the near vicinity, or to London, or indeed to any country in the world.

As the Industrial Revolution changed the face of British towns and cities, the paradox is that the dramatic effects of this trend towards urbanization fell unevenly. In the half century covered by this book, some hitherto important cities were left almost untouched, and were passed by; they were overtaken by previously less important centres, which developed out of all recognition. This selection of town plans clearly encapsulates this shift of balance between the pre-industrial centres, as depicted by Cole and Roper, and the new industrial centres of the Victorian period, mapped by Tallis.

It is to the Romans, those practical and methodical architects, that early English towns owe their design, characterized by two wide streets crossing at right angles at the centre of the town, with each street extending to a gate in the walled perimeter, exemplified by the ground plan of Chichester, evident in George Loader's survey of 1812. In this scheme, the streets bear simple identifying names: North Street, South Street, West Street and East Street, in Chichester's case, or Northgate, Southgate, and so on, in other circumstances.

In medieval times the pattern of the town organically, frequently centred around the castle or the cathedral. Here again, the names of the streets are more descriptive than imaginative, examples being High Street, Bridge Street, Castle Street and Horsefair.

The standard unit of local government in medieval England was the county, itself subdivided into smaller units, typically the hundred but rapes in Sussex, or lathes in Kent, for example. The focal point of the county was the county town; in many cases, the county town gave name to its county – for example, Bedford, Cambridge, Oxford, Worcester, Gloucester and Hereford. These centres were, in a predominantly agricultural economy, also important as centres of distribution. Both in the plans themselves and in the accompanying text there is evidence of this function: the market-place is featured prominently, and emphasis is given to the regular weekly market or markets and the larger, sometimes more specialized, fairs with regular annual dates, such as Nottingham's Goose Fair or Oxford's St Giles' Fair. This pattern and rhythm had continued unchanged for half a millennium. It is these county towns that formed the basis of Cole and Roper's set of town plans.

The Industrial Revolution caused the transformation of England from a largely peasant-agrarian economy into an industrial complex, focused in the new industrial centres. The new agricultural machinery increased production, but was less labour-intensive. Faced with rural unemployment, people in their thousands left the fields and migrated to urban centres to look for work.

One town of early eminence that was passed by was Hereford, a medieval city and capital of the Anglo-Saxon kingdom of Mercia, which today almost retains its pre-industrial nature, and which can be contrasted with Sheffield. Although long associated with iron smelting, Sheffield was on the verge of ruin, until the discovery of the South Yorkshire coal-field, and the change from water-power to steam, from which time the steel industry in Sheffield expanded rapidly. As a consequence, the population of Sheffield almost doubled in the two decades between 1831 and 1851. It is difficult to imagine Sheffield's advance, without the railway. For Hereford, however, final judgement was served by the railway companies, when the town was by-passed by the planners of the initial rail network, as depicted in Tallis's map.

The role of the railways in the transformation of Britain cannot be overestimated. The railways enabled manufacturers to move their products quickly and cheaply to the customer, obviating the need for an industry to be close to its markets. Although this was a boon to all industries, it was of particular importance for farmers, for the railways enabled them to move fresh produce further than ever before, to larger markets. This in turn also served to break the influence hitherto enjoyed by the smaller market towns, in favour of the developing urban industrial centres.

While not the first to be designed and made, George Stephenson's locomotive, built in 1818, provided the necessary means. On September 27th, 1825, the first passenger-carrying railway in the world, the Stockton and Darlington Railway, was opened. This railway was soon followed by others, both in England and in Scotland, including the Liverpool and Manchester Railway, opened in September, 1830, which was designed to carry not just produce and ores, but passengers as well.

Hand in hand with the Industrial Revolution, went a rise in the general affluence of the population, and an increase in leisure time. So, although the railway network was originally designed by companies for its application to commerce, it also enabled individuals, and their families, to travel away on excursion trips, or even holidays, most frequently to the coast. It was this movement that saw the development of coastal resorts, such as Brighton, Margate, Blackpool and Bangor. Prior to the railway, the common folk were simply not accustomed to moving far from their home village, with many people being born and dying, and spending the intervening years in the same parish.

Just as some inland cities failed to benefit from the Industrial Revolution, so, too, did some of the ports Bristol, the first sea-port of England in the Middle Ages, saw itself superseded by Liverpool in the first half of the nineteenth century, partly as a consequence of the latter's better harbour facilities, Liverpool's development to a position of pre-eminence started with the construction of the wet dock, designed by Thomas Steers in 1709, which used floodgates to overcome the problems of the tide. This, the first of its kind in the world, much expanded the city's dock facilities. Liverpool also proved to be better sited for the trade with America than Bristol, and began to overhaul its rival, but its proximity to the new industrial regions of the Midlands and North confirmed the new order.

By a combination of native industry and good fortune, Britain led the rest of the world into the New Industrial period, as Britain's work-force produced goods that markets in the rest of the world wished to buy. In 1835, for example, 60 per cent of the cotton goods consumed in the world were produced in England, and passed through England's docks, to be shipped to their destination.

As the population of the towns expanded, the medieval town plan was finally outgrown. Planned rows of housing, whether for artisans or the middle classes, were added on to the towns with a uniformity which still surprises visitors from overseas; and the nomenclature of British victories appears in street names such as Wellington, Nelson, Trafalgar and Waterloo throughout the towns and cities of the kingdom.

Maps and map-making

The technological advances brought by the Industrial Revolution also had their impact on map-making. The primary areas affected were the manufacture of paper, the printing press, and the printing plate itself. The new technology introduced paper-making machines, which could make paper faster and cheaper (though also of a lesser quality) than the hand-made method practised at the beginning of the century. Earliest versions of the steam-press could print four times faster than the old

JOHN TALLIS & JOHN RAPKIN

Railway Map of Great Britain

Tallis' railway map of Great Britain showing the railways completed, and the stations on each line, up to the present time, with the steamboat tracks from the principal British and Continental sea ports. Compiled from Government Documents, and the most recent Railway Information. By John Rapkin.

An important factor in the urbanization of England was the rapidly expanding railway network being established across the English countryside, as reflected in Tallis' map of the railways, published *c*.1855.

The Stockton and Darlington railway opened on September 27th, 1825, taking precedence as the first passenger-carrying railway in the world. Soon, other railways companies, both in England and Scotland, opened their own lines. In October, 1830 the Liverpool and Manchester railway was opened. This line was important as the first designed to carry not just produce and ores, but passengers as well. The railway was 31 miles long, with double line along the whole route. The journey took 90 minutes, at an average fare of about 5s.

The increase in the network was very rapid. In 1825, in England there were 25 miles of railway track; by 1844, this figure was 2,236; by 1850, 6,635, by 1860, 10,410, and by 1870 the figure had leaped to 15,310.

Just as the length of tracks rose, so too did the numbers of passengers. David Smith (*Victorian Maps of the British Isles*, p.100) notes that in 1850, 72.9 million passengers (and this not including season-ticket holders) travelled on the railways. In 1860, this figure had jumped to 163.4 million, in 1870, 336.5 million, and by 1880 the total had reached 603.9 million people.

In 1851, during the Great Exhibition, one London terminus station, Euston, handled three quarters of a million passengers.

The transformation induced by the railway network must have been as startling to the people of early nineteenth-century Britain as the figures are today.

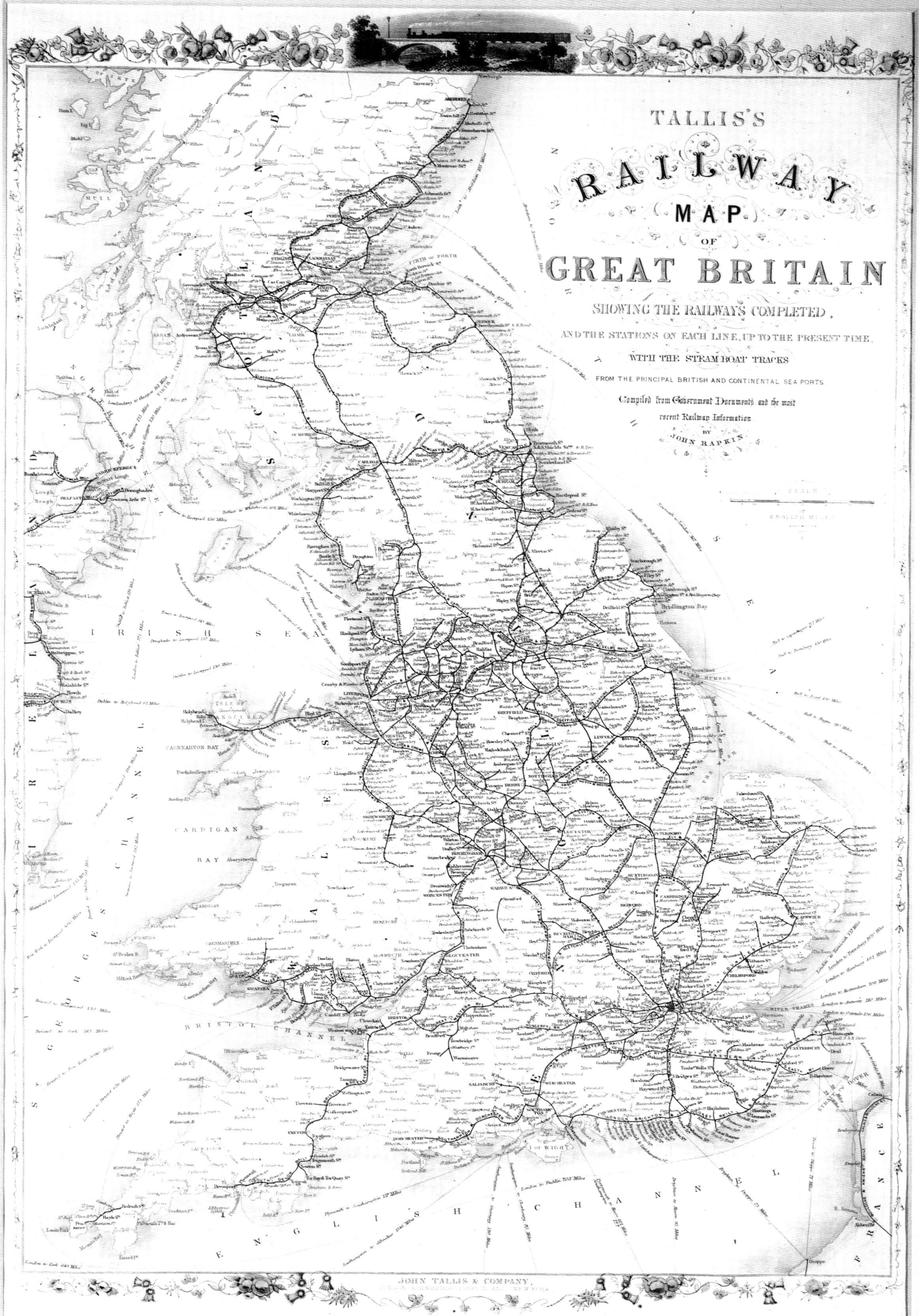

TALLIS'S RAILWAY MAP OF GREAT BRITAIN

SHOWING THE RAILWAYS COMPLETED,

AND THE STATIONS ON EACH LINE, UP TO THE PRESENT TIME,

WITH THE STEAM BOAT TRACKS

FROM THE PRINCIPAL BRITISH AND CONTINENTAL SEA PORTS.

Compiled from Government Documents and the most recent Railway Information

BY

JOHN RAPKIN

SCALE OF ENGLISH MILES

JOHN TALLIS & COMPANY,

hand-press. The effect was to make printing cheaper. All that was necessary was a more suitable printing plate.

At the beginning of the nineteenth century, printing plates were made from thin sheets of copper, on to which the image would be engraved. This was an intaglio process, which means that the picture was cut into the plate with an engraving tool or acid. When completed, the plate would be inked, and then wiped with a cloth, to remove the ink from the polished surface, but leaving ink in the engraved grooves in the plate. Then the paper would be placed over the plate in a press, which exerted great pressure, forcing the two together, and transferring the ink on to the paper. Copper had been the metal used since 1477, when the first atlas was printed. It had the advantage of being a soft metal, so it could be engraved easily, but its softness also made it susceptible to wear, particularly because of the pressure it was subjected to in the press, after only a few hundred examples had been printed. Once this happened, the plate would have to be reworked to strengthen the engraved lines, a laborious process. In all, perhaps only round about one or at most two thousand examples could be printed from a copper plate.

In the 1820s, publishers started using steel plates instead. Steel had the benefit of being much harder, and more durable, so that much larger numbers of examples could be printed. A skilled engraver could also produce a finer line on a steel plate, a great benefit for clarity and quality of engraving. The main drawback was that it was more difficult to engrave a steel plate, or to revise and correct it, if necessary.

At the same time, a new process was being developed: lithography. This process used a porous stone, often limestone. The picture would be drawn on with wax, almost like a modern crayon. The whole surface would then be dampened. The exposed face of the stone would absorb the water, but the wax would repel it. Then, when the stone was inked, the ink would adhere only to the wax. This process had numbers of advantages; in particular, there was very little wear and tear to the stone during printing, so even larger numbers of examples could be produced. Also, it was far easier to amend the image, so as to insert new information, as appropriate.

In books of this kind, very often the publishers would cull existing sources for text and maps; this series is remarkable in that Brayley, the principal author, endeavoured to travel to the places he was writing about. In the first four years, Britton and Brayley travelled over 3,500 miles, carrying out their research. Equally, the plans seem to be completely original works, taken from original surveys carried out for the volume, and not reworkings of existing material, which adds considerably to their historical value.

The plans are copper-plate engravings, each measuring approximately 180 × 235mm.

The series of plans:

G. Cole & J. Roper

From: 'The British Atlas: Comprising a Complete Set of County Maps, of England and Wales; with a General Map of Navigable Rivers and Canals; and Plans of Cities and Principal Towns.'

This collection of twenty-one plans was drawn under the direction of Edward Brayley, by G. Cole, and engraved by J. Roper. The series was originally prepared for John Britton and Edward Brayley's *The Beauties of England and Wales*, a compendious twenty-five-volume description of England and Wales, county by county. Because of the expense of such a large undertaking, which was originally expected to be only six volumes, the publishers, Vernor and Hood, issued the series in monthly parts. The first part was published on April 1st, 1801. In an original advertisement announcing the project, the publishers said each part would contain 80 pages of text, and three views of prominent buildings, priced 2s. 6d. Also prepared for the book were maps of the individual counties, and these town plans.

Thomas Moule

Thomas Moule (1784–1851) is celebrated as the last English map-maker to blend together both geographical and decorative features on his county maps, in the face of the rise of the Ordnance Survey. The

Ordnance Survey, whose maps eschewed such antiquarian 'fripperies' in the pursuit of modern geographic and scientific excellence, chose to map England on a national grid, so their maps ignored the division of England into county units.

His maps were issued in parts between 1830 and 1836, each accompanied by a section of descriptive text relating to the county. When the series was complete, the maps and texts were issued as the *English Counties Delineated*, published in 1837. Apart from maps of the various counties, Moule included plans of London, Bath, Boston in Lincolnshire, Oxford and Cambridge, all reproduced here.

As an author of a *Bibliotheca Heraldica*, and author and contributor to works on English and Continental architecture, and to Westall's *Great Britain Illustrated*, Moule brought a number of varied and fascinating interests to this series, which were blended together, in the visual design of the maps.

Of all the maps in the series, arguably the plan of Oxford is the most striking, and provides evidence of Moule's many facets. In the blank areas around the simple street plans are the arms of the various Oxford Colleges; below the plan are views of the city from the north, and of Christ Church College.

This happy, and judicious, blend helps explain the popularity this series enjoyed both in its own day, and also among modern admirers and collectors. Being printed from steel plates, and produced in large numbers, they are readily found today.

Robert Kearsley Dawson

One of the largest series of plans of the cities and towns of England and Wales was prepared by Robert Dawson, from 1832 onwards. Although not strictly street maps in the way the Cole and Roper, Moule and Tallis maps are, Dawson's series is particularly important in the history of the development of the towns and cities, and in British political history.

The voting system that existed at the start of the nineteenth century was the result of haphazard and piecemeal evolution over many centuries. The result

was a system ruled by anomalies and haunted by corrupt practices. For example, those excluded from voting (and from holding office) were not only children, lunatics and convicted criminals, but also women, Nonconformists, Roman Catholics, Quakers, Jews and agnostics. Then, individual boroughs could have their own, additional, rules, to determine eligibility to vote.

Furthermore, it has been estimated that in 1793, with a population of 8,500,000 people, 257 of the 513 MPs representing England and Wales were returned by only 11,075 voters; 51 constituencies had under 50 voters, and 130 boroughs had under 300 voters. In particular, the voting system favoured established boroughs, and did not take into account population shifts. Thus, Cornwall, which paid 16 out of 513 parts of the land-tax, returned 42 MPs, while Lancashire, which paid ten times as much, had 16 MPs. Both Birmingham and Manchester went unrepresented, while the borough of Dunwich, which was half under the sea, had two MPs, one for every seven voters.

In 1832, Parliament acknowledged these failings, and passed the Reform Bill, which established the mechanism for a complete overhaul of the electoral system. The primary step was the complete revision of existing constituency boundaries. Commissioners were appointed to draw up a report, *Municipal Corporation Boundaries (England and Wales)*, which laid down the new constituency boundaries. These reports were accompanied by the series of maps by Dawson, to show these proposed boundaries. It is these reports and maps that laid the basis for the modern parliamentary constituencies of the British Parliament.

The Society for the Diffusion of Useful Knowledge

One of the most fascinating features of Victorian England is the number of benevolent, almost paternalistic, societies that sought to disseminate knowledge throughout society, aimed particularly at the poor.

The Society was founded by John, Earl Russell, and Henry Brougham, later Lord Chancellor of England, in 1827. Earl Russell, a distinguished parliamentarian, had a keen interest in culture for the people. Through his work in Parliament, he secured an additional grant of £30,000 for education, and was responsible for securing an inspectorate for schools.

Under their leadership, the Society published numbers of books that were good quality, but competitively priced, so as to be affordable. Perhaps the grandest of their publications was their atlas of the world, entitled *Maps of the Society for the Diffusion of Useful Knowledge*, published by Baldwin and Cradock in 1833–4 and later reissued by Chapman and Hall.

Within this important atlas was a series of plans of towns and cities of the world; the British towns included were London, Birmingham, Dublin, Edinburgh and Liverpool.

Although functional plans, these steel engravings are enlivened with small vignettes comparing the height of principal buildings of the city, and in Liverpool's case, a finely engraved view.

John Wood

John Wood was a Yorkshire surveyor who based himself in Edinburgh, following his marriage to a local girl. Wood was one of the most ambitious surveyors of the day, travelling widely, at first in Scotland, but then through northern England and Wales, surveying towns, before returning to Edinburgh to see the plans through the press.

This group of four plans of Wales was prepared and published in 1834, as separate issues. In contrast to the plans by Cole and Roper, Moule and Tallis, these were functional items, not book illustrations. This is exemplified by the large scale on which they were prepared, and the vast amount of detail they contain on property and land ownership.

As separate publications, and functional items, these sheets were not afforded the protection of book covers that the other series enjoyed, hence the visible signs of damage to the margins and borders. The survival rate of such sheets is extremely low, so often the only surviving examples are not found in such good condition as comparable atlas maps.

John Tallis

This large collection of town plans of British cities was issued to accompany re-issues of Montgomery Martin's *The Illustrated Atlas And Modern History Of The World*, in a companion volume entitled *Index-Gazetteer Of The World: . . . Illustrated With Plans of the Principal Towns in Great Britain, America &c. Drawn and Engraved From The Most Recent Government Surveys, and Other Authentic Documents*, published by John Tallis, after whom these maps and plans are most popularly known.

The series, originally issued in serial form, was published in 1851, to coincide with the Great Exhibition, although the town plans were added later, perhaps in about 1855.

The series is notable as being the last series of visually decorative maps of the world; Tallis endeavoured to fill the maps with small vignettes depicting local people, their towns, landmarks, and animals and birds, to bring the country depicted to life for his British audience. In the same way, his fine set of city plans highlights the prominent buildings, antiquities, monuments, bridges and other structures.

The steel-plate engravings of the series exemplify what a competent engraver could achieve, with the delicate frame surrounds and precise detail visible in the vignettes.

Conclusion

If, looking back, it appears that the towns of the British Isles changed so dramatically in the first half of the nineteenth century, then how much more evident is the contrast between these plans and the cities as they now exist at the close of the twentieth century. These charming historical artefacts provide a fascinating visual record of a bygone time. Although produced with increasingly modern technology, these plans retain an antiquarian feel; yet, this same modern technology enabled their production in numbers large enough to make them readily available, and affordable, for the modern private collector.

TOWN
AND
CITY MAPS
OF THE BRITISH ISLES

1880-1855

THE PLATES

Bedford

Bedford is the county town of Bedfordshire, centrally sited within the county, and situated fifty miles from London, on the River Ouse. The population is 5,546 (1831).

Built at a ford over the navigable river, Bedford derives its name from the Saxon 'Bedicanford', meaning 'fortress on the ford'.

There was a destructive fire in the north part of the town in 1802, since which time great improvements have taken place.

Here is much business done in the corn trade, the neighbourhood of the town being singularly productive in wheat and barely; the former of which is chiefly conveyed to the markets of Hitchin and Hertford, and then ground into meal, and sent to London. The trade in coal, malt, timber, and iron, between Bedford and Lynn, is also very considerable, by means of the navigation of the Ouse.

The town was one of the early centres of the lace trade, to the success of which French refugees in the seventeenth and eighteenth centuries largely contributed.

Markets are held on Mondays for pigs, and on Saturdays for corn &c.

The congregational chapel, of the 'Old Meeting', stands on the site of the building in which John Bunyan preached from 1656 onwards. Bedford is noted for its grammar school founded by Edward VI in 1552, and endowed by Sir William Harper.

(BEDFORD)

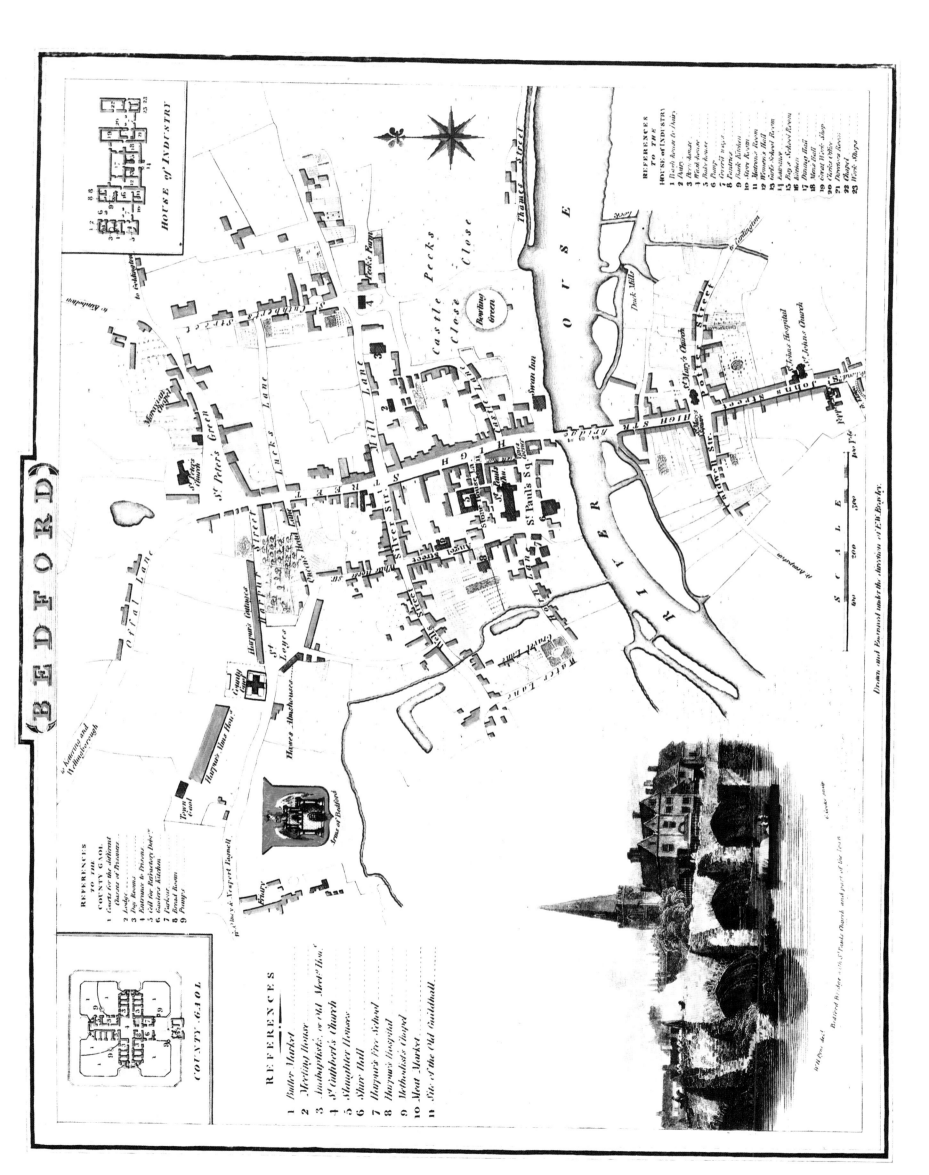

HOUSE of INDUSTRY

REFERENCES
To THE
HOUSE of INDUSTRY

1 Dwel: house to Insp:
2 Privy
3 Bys: house
4 Weak house
5 Bath house
6 Pump
7 Gravel ways
8 Fountain
9 Back Kitchen
10 Store Room
11 Matrons Room
12 Womens Hall
13 Girls School Room
14 Laundry
15 Boy's School Room
16 Kitchen
17 Dining Hall
18 Mens Hall
19 Great Work Shop
20 Porters Lodge
21 Provision Room
22 Chapel
23 Work Shops

REFERENCES
TO THE
COUNTY GAOL

1 Courts for the different
2 Lodge } Classes of Prisoners
3 Day Rooms
4 Entrance to Prisons
5 Cell for Refractory Debtor
6 Gaolers Kitchen
7 Parlour
8 Bread Room
9 Pumps

COUNTY GAOL

REFERENCES

1 Butter Market
2 Meeting House
3 Inabaptists, or Old Meet: House
4 St Cuthberts Church
5 Slaughter Houses
6 Shire Hall
7 Harpurs Free School
8 Harpurs Hospital
9 Methodists Chapel
10 Meat Market
11 Site of the Old Guildhall

SCALE

Drawn and Engraved under the direction of E.W. Brayley.

Cambridge

The county town of the county, and home of the University, is situated 50 miles from London, on the River Cam, and has a population of 9,273.

Cambridge occupies a perfect level, encompassed by the colleges, and their beautiful plantations and gardens on both sides of the Cam. Several of the streets are narrow and winding, but three of them are spacious and airy.

The market-place, which consists of two oblong squares, is spacious and centrally situated. At the upper end stands the shire hall, where the county assizes are held, at the back of which is the town hall. Fronting the shire hall is Hobson's Conduit, the gift of a rich Hackney-man in the reign of James I, whose tenacity in letting out his horses in strict rotation gave rise to the proverb of 'Hobson's choice'.

The town of Cambridge, as to business, is chiefly supported by the University; and the constant demand of articles of convenience and necessity by the numerous students. There is no manufacturing meriting description; but some trade is carried on in corn, oil and iron. The markets, which are under the control of the University, are amply supplied; and the butter, for which the vicinity is celebrated, is rolled up into such a form, as to sell by the yard, which is equivalent to the weight of a pound.

An annual fair is held near Barnwell, on a common called Midsummer Green; which is proclaimed on Midsummer-eve, by the heads of the University, and the mayor and corporation, and lasts three days. It is usually called the Pot-fair, owing to the articles for sale formerly consisting chiefly of earthenware.

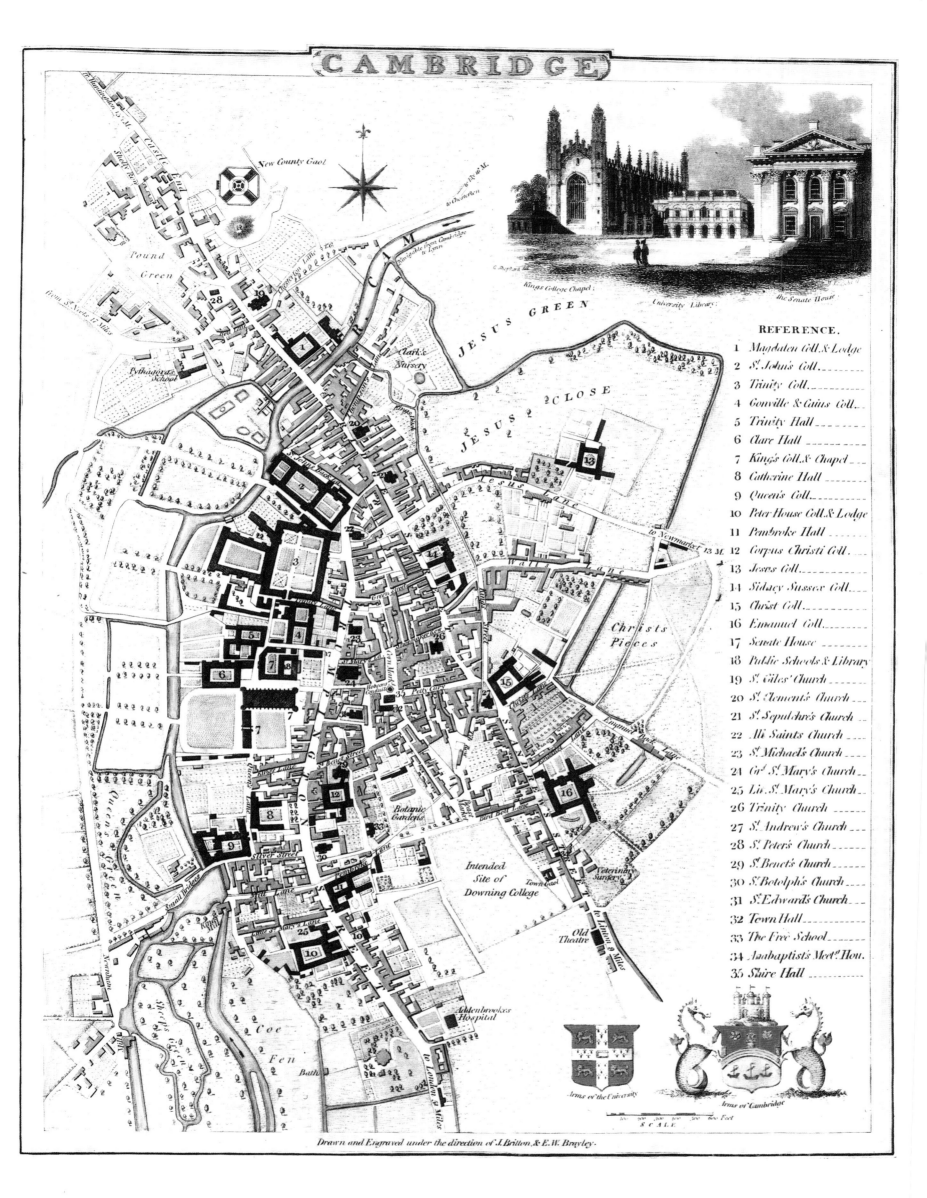

CAMBRIDGE

Kings College Chapel.

University Library.

the Senate House.

New County Gaol

to Oakington

to R. & M.

R. CAM

Navigable from Cambridge to Lynn

JESUS GREEN

JESUS CLOSE

Pound Green

From St Neots 17 Miles

Clark's Nursery

Jesus Lane

to Newmarket 13 M.

Walls Lane

Christ's Pieces

Queen's Green

Botanic Gardens

Rose Market

Bird Bolt Lane

Emanuel Road Way

Intended Site of Downing College

Town Gaol

Veterinary Surgery

Old Theatre

to Linton 9 Miles

Silver Street

Small Bridges

Kings Mill

Newnham

Addenbrookes Hospital

Coe Fen

Bath

to London 9 Miles

Sheeps Green

REFERENCE.

1 Magdalen Coll. & Lodge
2 St John's Coll.
3 Trinity Coll.
4 Gonville & Caius Coll.
5 Trinity Hall
6 Clare Hall
7 King's Coll. & Chapel
8 Catharine Hall
9 Queen's Coll.
10 Peter-House Coll. & Lodge
11 Pembroke Hall
12 Corpus Christi Coll.
13 Jesus Coll.
14 Sidney Sussex Coll.
15 Christ Coll.
16 Emanuel Coll.
17 Senate House
18 Public Schools & Library
19 St Giles' Church
20 St Clement's Church
21 St Sepulchre's Church
22 All Saints Church
23 St Michael's Church
24 Gr.t St Mary's Church
25 Lit. St Mary's Church
26 Trinity Church
27 St Andrew's Church
28 St Peter's Church
29 St Benet's Church
30 St Botolph's Church
31 St Edward's Church
32 Town Hall
33 The Free School
34 Anabaptist's Meet.g Hou.
35 Shire Hall

Arms of the University

Arms of Cambridge

SCALE

Drawn and Engraved under the direction of J. Britton & E.W. Brayley.

Canterbury

A city constituting a city and a county in itself, under the name of the city and county of the city of Canterbury, situated in Kent, seat of the Archbishop of Canterbury, 55 miles from London, with a population of 11,413.

The city is seated in a pleasant valley, surrounded with gently rising hills, from which flow several fine springs of water. It is also romantically watered by the River Stour, which divides itself into several small streams and forms islands of different sizes, on one of which the western part of the city is situated.

The city is of an oval shape, and the four principal streets are disposed in the form of a cross with a great number of smaller streets, lanes and alleys. The Guildhall is a handsome edifice, and there are elegant and commodious assembly rooms, a very neat theatre, a public library, a scientific institution with a museum, and an agricultural association.

The cattle market has been held on the site of the city moat from time immemorial. The provision and fish markets, which are very plentifully provided, are situated near the gate of the cathedral.

The asylum afforded here to the persecuted Walloons, and to the French Protestants, on the revocation of the Edict of Nantes, produced something like a revival, by the introduction of silk-weaving by those industrious refugees. This business has in turn given way to the cotton, and silk and cotton manufacture of a description of piece goods which receive the name of Canterbury and Chamberry muslins, damasks, &c. The culture of hops being carried out all round the city, it is rendered one of the first hop-markets in England; it has also been celebrated from time immemorial for the excellence of its brawn. Here are two mineral springs which are celebrated for their medicinal qualities, with very convenient subscription baths.

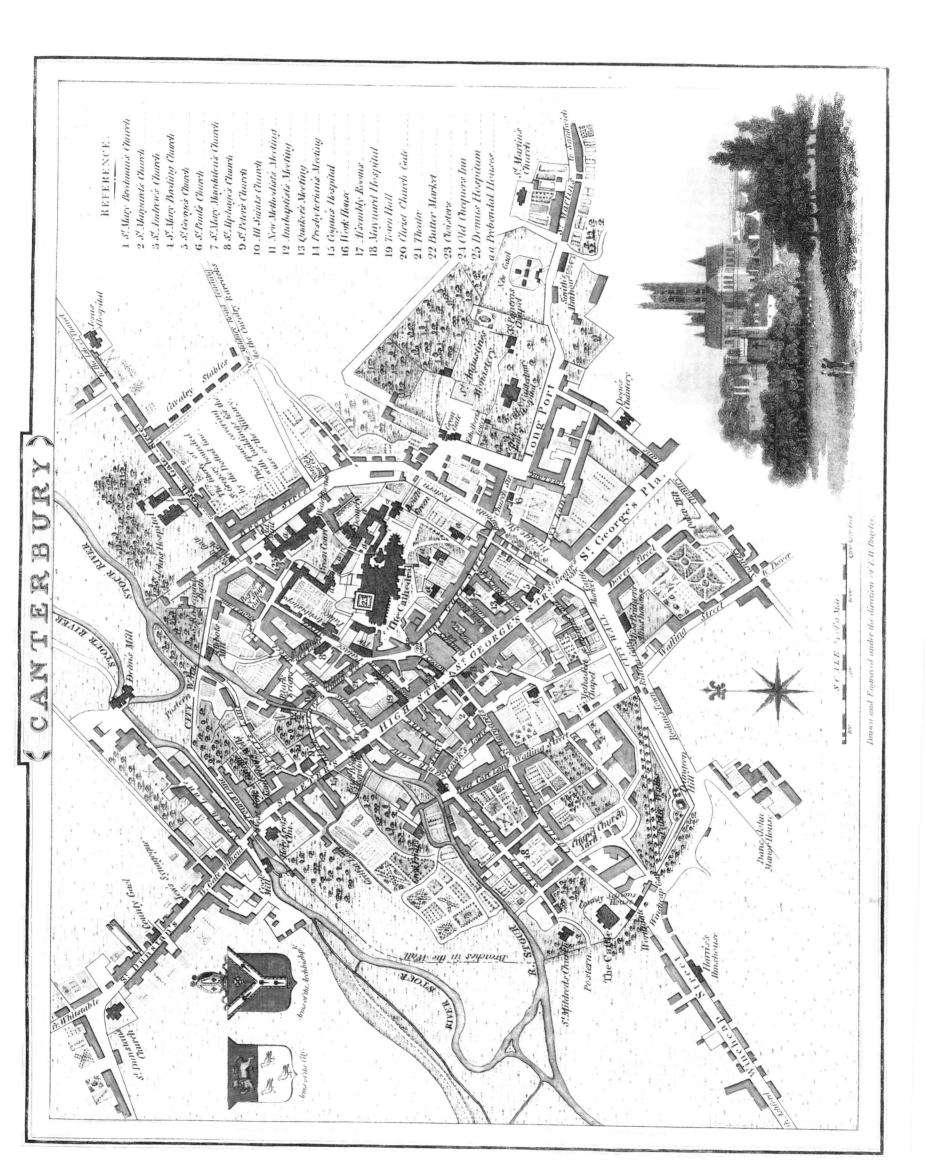

⟨ C A N T E R B U R Y ⟩

REFERENCE.

1 St. Mary Bredman's Church
2 St. Margaret's Church
3 St. Andrew's Church
4 St. Mary Bredin Church
5 St. George's Church
6 St. Pauls Church
7 St. Mary Magdalen's Church
8 St. Alphage's Church
9 St. Peter's Church
10 All Saints Church
11 New Methodists Meeting
12 Anabaptists Meeting
13 Quakers Meeting
14 Presbyterians Meeting
15 Cogan's Hospital
16 Work House
17 Assembly Rooms
18 Maynard Hospital
19 Town Hall
20 Christ Church Gate
21 Theatre
22 Butter Market
23 Cloisters
24 Old Chequers Inn
25 Dennis Hospitum
aa Prebendal Houses

Drawn and Engraved under the direction of E.W. Brayley.

Carlisle

Carlisle is an ancient city and the capital of the county, it occupies a gentle eminence at the confluence of the Eden and Calder, 301 miles from London, and has a population of 10,225.

The principal streets of Carlisle diverge from the market place and are called English Street, Scotch Street and Castle Street, all of which are broad and spacious.

The manufactures consist chiefly of cotton yarn, cotton ginghams and checks, Osnaburghs, drills, worsted shags, stamped cottons, superior hats, shamoy tanned-leather lindsays, nails, hardware, flax and ropes. The markets are abundantly supplied with provisions and excellent fish. Much business is also done at the various fairs, and during those held in August, for horned cattle and linen, and September for horses and horned cattle, all persons are free from arrest in this city, agreeably to the terms of an ancient charter.

Races are also held annually on a fine course on the south side of the Eden, the first King's Plate being given in 1763.

Nothing can be more pleasant than the vicinity of this city; the inhabitants with well-judged charity having employed a number of poor people during a dearth of employment to improve the roads, and form handsome walks all around it.

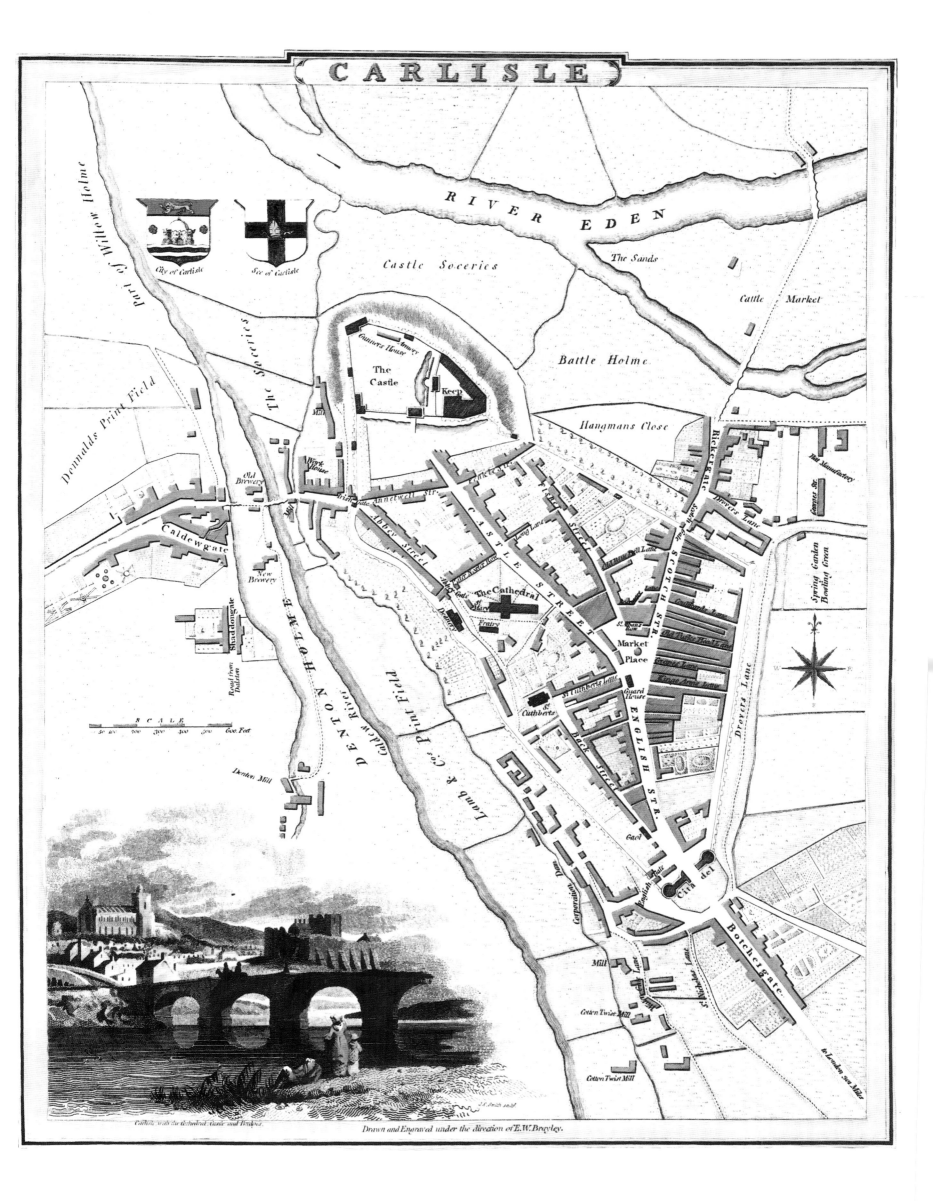

CARLISLE

RIVER EDEN

The Sands

Castle Soceries

Cattle Market

Part of Willow Holme

City of Carlisle

See of Carlisle

The Soceries

Battle Holme

Gunners House   Armory

The Castle   Keep

Hangmans Close

Bickergate

Drovers Lane

Fat Manufactory

Hannes Str

Dennalds Print Field

Mill

Work House

Old Brewery

Bristo Gate Annetwell Str.

Abbey Street

Long Lane   Fisher Street

Castle Street

SCOTCH STR.

Spring Garden
Bowling Green

Caldewgate

New Brewery

Shaddongate

Road from Dalston

Denton Mill

DENTON HOLME

Caldew River

Lamb & Co's Pint Field

The Cathedral

Friary

Market Place

ENGLISH STR.

St Cuthbert Lane

Guard House

Drovers Lane

Back Street

St Cuthberts

SCALE
50 100 200 300 400 500 600 Feet

Gaol

Mill

Coperation Lane

St Nicholas Lane

English Gate

Cita del

Botchergate

Cotton Twist Mill

Cotton Twist Mill

to London 301 Miles

Carlisle with the Cathedral Castle and Bridges.

J.C. Smith sculp.

Drawn and Engraved under the direction of E.W. Brayley.

Chester

The county town of Cheshire, a large and ancient city, seated on the Dee, 183 miles from London, with a population of 19,949.

The city is half encircled by a sweep of the River Dee, hence its Roman name of Deva. This name was subsequently relinquished for that of 'Cestria' from Castrium, a military station. The walls of the present city determine the limits of the ancient walls and even the buildings are disposed in the form of a Roman camp, consisting principally of four streets running from a common centre to the cardinal points of the compass.

These streets have been excavated from a stratum of rock, and in consequence are sunken several feet below the natural surface, a circumstance which has produced a singular construction of the houses. On the level of the street are low shops and warehouses, and above them a gallery on each side reaching from street to street open in front and balustrated. These galleries, called 'rows', appear exceeding curious to strangers, as they seem to be formed through the first floors of the houses.

Chester may be deemed a sort of provincial metropolis for the gentry of the neighbouring counties of moderate fortune. Its maritime trade is chiefly coasting and with Ireland, whence great quantities of linen are imported. Besides linen, wood, hides, tallow, feathers, butter, provisions and other articles are received from Ireland; grocery from London, timber from Wales; hemp, flax and iron from the Baltic; and fruit, oil, barilla, cork and wine from Spain and Portugal. The exports are coal, lead, calomine, copper-plates, cast-iron and vast quantities of cheese. The only manufacture of any consequence is that of gloves.

Annual races commencing the first Monday in May are run on the Roodeye, a fine level course beneath the city walls, from which the races are to be seen to great advantage.

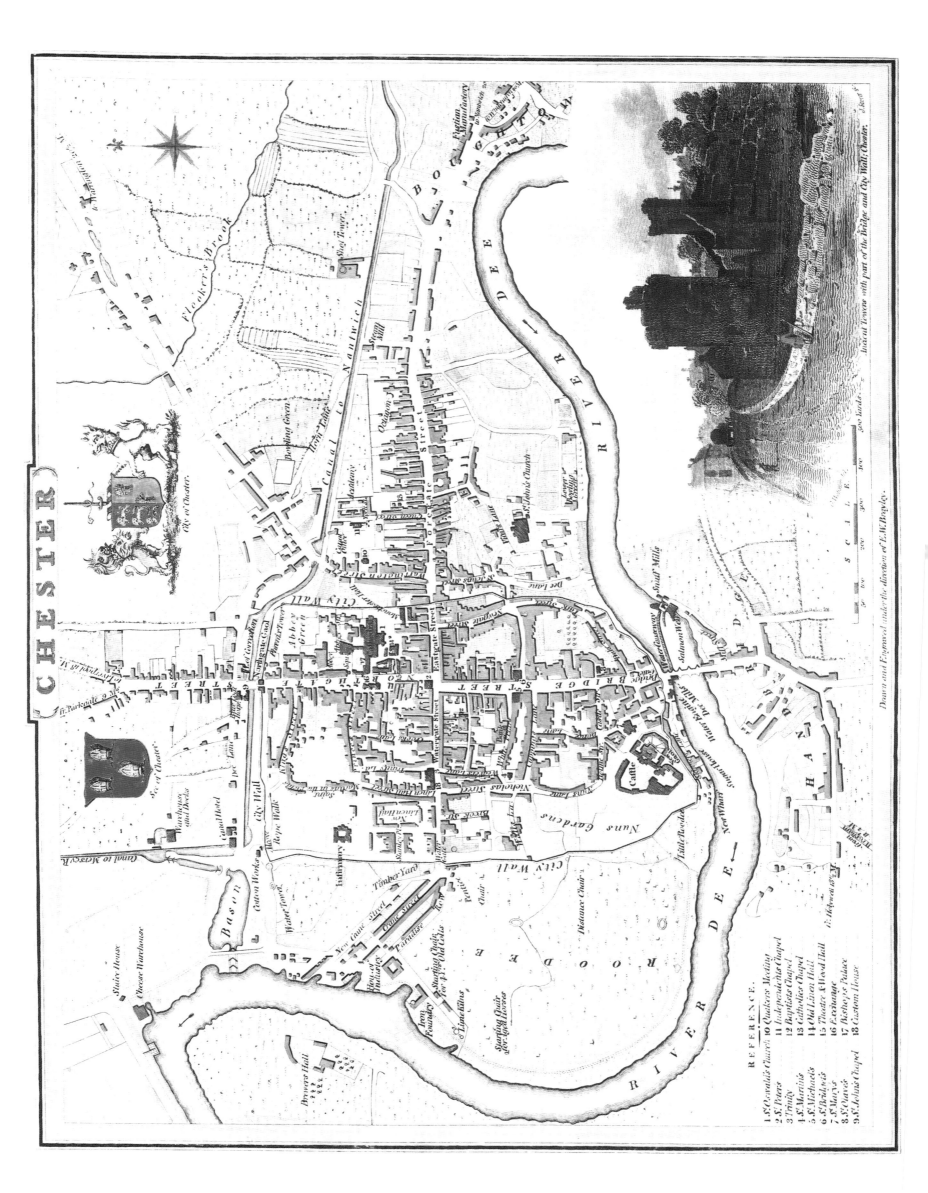

(CHESTER)

REFERENCE.

1 St Oswald's Church
2 St Peter
3 Trinity
4 St Martins
5 St Michaels
6 St Bridget's
7 St Mary's
8 St Olaves
9 St John's Chapel
10 Quakers Meeting
11 Independents Chapel
12 Baptists Chapel
13 Catholics Chapel
14 Old Linen Hall
15 Theatre & Wood Hall
16 Exchange
17 Bishop's Palace
18 Custom House

Drawn and Engraved under the direction of L. W. Bagley.

Ancient Towers, with part of the Bridge and City Walls, Chester.

Colchester

Colchester lies 51 miles from London, and has a population of 10,089. A large and populous borough and market town of great antiquity, it is chiefly built on the northern declivity of a hill, rising from the banks of the River Coln. Colchester is with great probability supposed to have been an ancient British settlement before the invasion of this island by the Romans. Though history may reject the story of King Cole, yet it is certain that this town was one of the most important establishments of the Romans so long as they continued masters of this country.

The streets are regular and well built throughout the principal part of the town. There is a large and convenient market-place, where fairs are held on Easter Tuesday for woollens, 5th of July for horses, 23rd of July for cattle and horses, and 20th of October for cattle, horses, butter and toys.

The River Coln is navigable for small craft up to a place called the Hithe, within three miles of the town, where there is a quay and a custom house.

The principal manufacture is of a kind of coarse woollens called beizes and serges, said to have been introduced here in the reign of Queen Elizabeth. This trade is under the control of a Corporation of the Governors of the Dutch Beize-Hall, whose officers have authority to examine the cloth previous to its sale. Among the articles of produce for which Colchester has been noted are candied eryingo roots and oysters, of which last, quantities are sent to London and elsewhere.

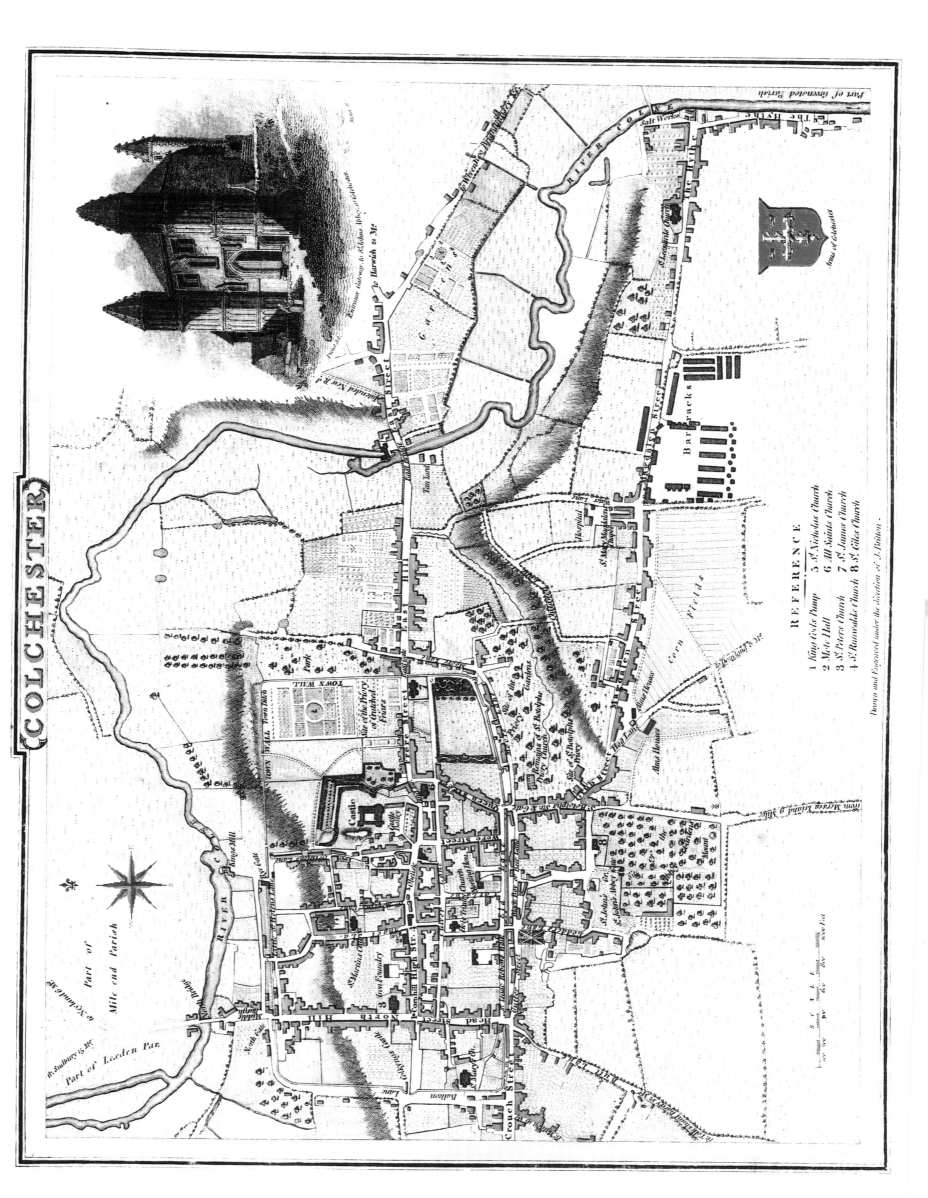

COLCHESTER

Part of Greensted Parish

The HYDE

RIVER COLNE

Salt Works

St Leonards Church

Barracks

Part of Leeden Par.

Part of Mile end Parish

To Sudbury 15 M.

To St Nichola 6 M.

RIVER

Kings Mill

North Gate

NORTH HILL

Crouch Street

Balcon Lane

St Mary's Clo.

St Johns Abbey Gate

Abbey Gardens

Mount

Ryegate

Castle

Castle Bailey

TOWN WALL

TOWN DITCH

Park

Site of the Priory of Crutched Friars

St Peters Church

Remains of St Botolphs Priory

Site of St Botolphs Priory

Magdalen Str.

St Mary Magdalen Church

Hospital

Hythe Str.

Garden

Founded New R.d

To Harwich 21 M.

Eastmore Gateway, to S.John's Abbey, at Colchester.

Arms of Colchester

REFERENCE

1 King Cole's Pump   5 St Nicholas Church
2 Mote Hall   6 All Saints Church
3 St Peters Church   7 St James Church
4 St Runwalds Church   8 St Giles Church

Drawn and Engraved under the direction of J. Britton.

SCALE

from Mersea Island 9 Miles

to Langham 3 M.

Corn fields

Alms Houses

Alms Houses

Coventry

Coventry lies 91 miles from London, and has a population of 17,923 (1811). A city, and in conjunction with Lichfield, the see of a bishop. It stands in the centre of the kingdom, and is principally built on a declivity, about three quarters of a mile in length, watered by the Rivers Radford and Sherborn. The streets in general are narrow, and the domestic architecture chiefly of an ancient character. It has some claim to great antiquity, but its authentic history cannot be traced higher than the beginning of the 11th century. Woollen cloth, caps, and bonnets were made at Coventry in the beginning of the 15th century and the woollen manufacture continued to flourish till the destruction of the Turkey trade towards the end of the 17th century.

At present Coventry is noted for the manufacture of ribbons and watches; the former was introduced about a century ago and it is become so extensive, that in 1801 there were 2,819 silk and ribbon-looms in the vicinity. Watch-making was introduced here within the last forty years; and at present more watches, it is said, are made here than in the metropolis. The water of the River Sherborn is famed for its excellence as a medium for dyeing blue. Commerce is facilitated by the construction of the Oxford and Coventry Canal, which, communicating with the Grand Trunk Navigation, affords the means of transporting goods to almost every part of the kingdom.

Coventry has been peculiarly fortunate in escaping conflagration, and in consequence it presents the aspect of a city of the seventeenth century.

The legendary generosity of the Countess Godiva to the men of Coventry has been perpetuated by an annual procession on May 2nd, in which one of the principal characters is 'Peeping-Tom', the indiscreet and inquisitive tailor. The Godiva procession is still continued at Coventry, though its commencement dates only from the reign of Charles II.

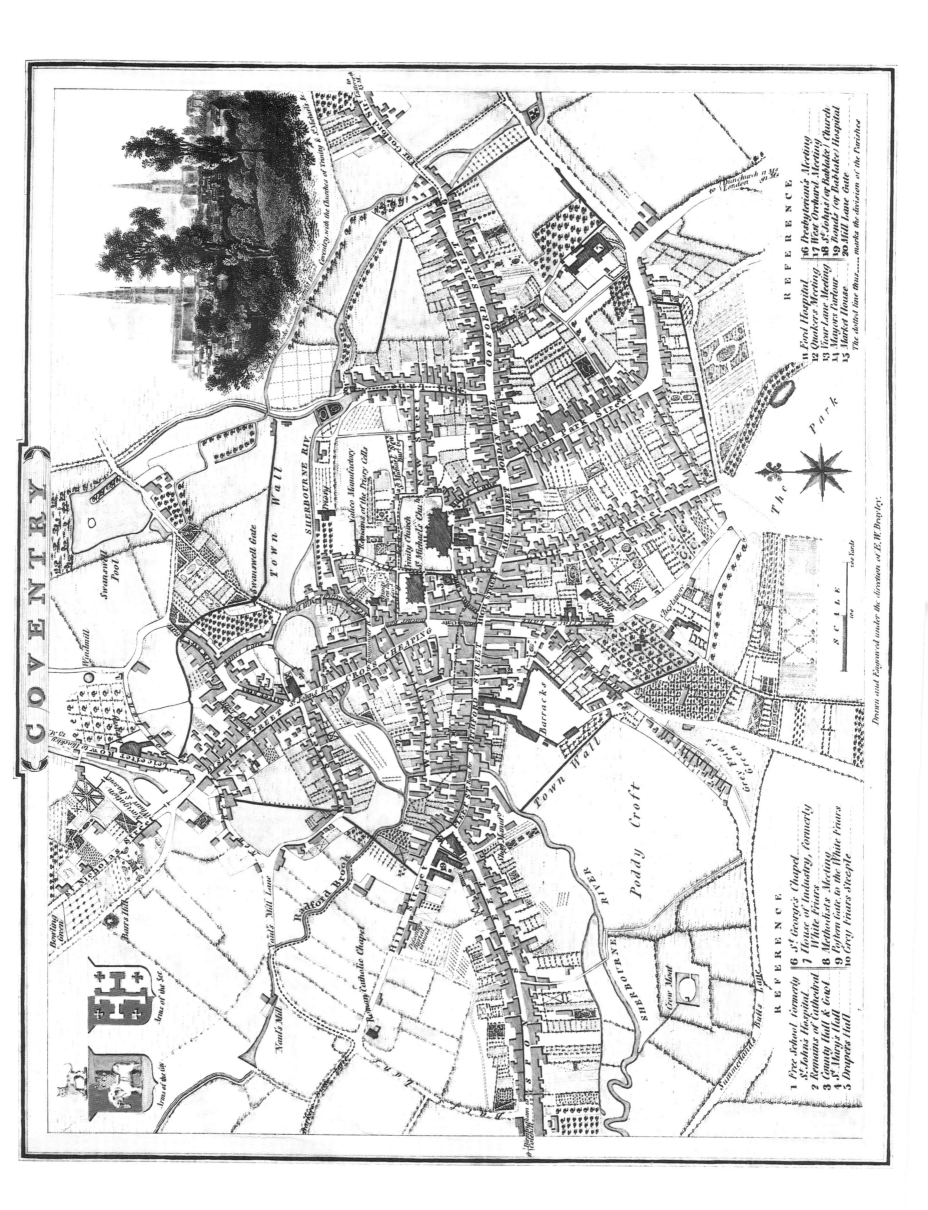

COVENTRY

REFERENCE

1 Free School, formerly
2 St. John's Hospital
3 Remains of Cathedral
4 County Hall & Gaol
5 St. Mary's Hall
6 Draper's Hall

6 St. George's Chapel
7 House of Industry, formerly
  White Friars
8 Methodists Meeting
9 Pybern Gate to the White Friars
10 Grey Friars Steeple

REFERENCE

11 Ford Hospital
12 Quakers Meeting
13 Vicar Lane Meeting
14 Mayor's Parlour
15 Market House

16 Presbyterian's Meeting
17 West Orchard Meeting
18 St. John's or Bablake Church
19 Bonds (or Bablake) Hospital
20 Mill Lane Gate

The dotted line thus....... marks the division of the Parishes

Drawn and Engraved under the direction of E. W. Brayley.

Derby

The county town of Derbyshire, Derby is situated 126 miles from London, and has a population of 10,728.

This town comprises many handsome houses of modern erection as well as some good public buildings. The streets are spacious and well paved, and through a considerable part of the town flows a stream, called Markerton Brook, over which there are five stone bridges. Among the principal public edifices are the Assembly Room on the east of the market place, erected by subscription about 1774, and the Guildhall built by the Corporation about 1730. A free school has been founded here at which the celebrated astronomer Flamstead is said to have been educated.

The Derbyshire General Infirmary is one of the noblest structures of the kind in England, completed for the reception of patients in 1800, at the expense of £17,870 including the price paid for the ground on which it stands. This place was formerly a great wool-mart; and the art of dyeing woollen cloth was supposed to be practised here with peculiar advantage, in consequence of the water of the Derwent being especially adapted for that purpose.

Derby ale is mentioned by Camden in the reign of Elizabeth, and a century later the town retained its reputation for making malt and malt liquor. It has long been famous for its silk-works. In 1814 there were ten in the town, affording employment to about 1,200 persons. The porcelain manufacture was introduced in about 1750 and the articles produced are said to surpass the finest of foreign workmanship. Fluorspar, marble, and alabaster are here manufactured into a variety of articles, useful and ornamental.

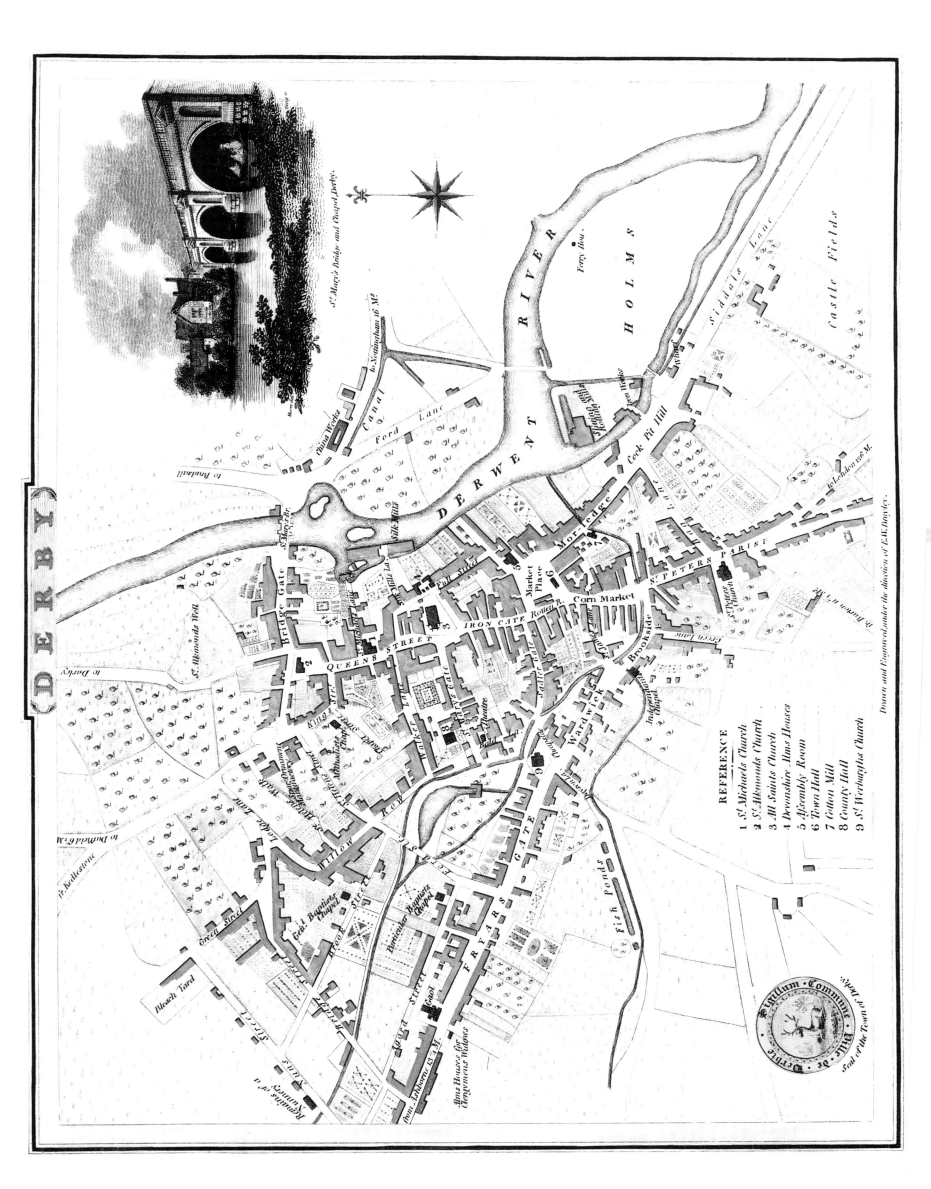

DERBY

REFERENCE
1 St Michaels Church
2 St Alkmonds Church
3 All Saints Church
4 Devonshire Alms Houses
5 Assembly Room
6 Town Hall
7 Cotton Mill
8 County Hall
9 St Werburghs Church

Drawn and Engraved, under the direction of E. W. Brayley.

St Mary's Bridge and Chapel Derby.

Sigillum Commune Burgi de Derby.
Seal of the Town of Derby.

Durham

The county town of the county of the same name, Durham lies 258 miles from London, and has a population of 7,530.

An ancient city, the capital of the county, it is irregularly built on a rocky eminence, almost encompassed by the Wear. The highest ground in the centre is occupied by the cathedral and castle which, with the streets called The Baileys, are included within the limits of the old walls of the city.

The market place is a small quadrangle, having in the centre a conduit to supply the inhabitants with water, on the south side a piazza where the corn market is held, and on the west the Guildhall. The central conduit is an octagon building, surmounted by a statue of Neptune, and the water is conveyed from a spring about half a mile distant. A new and handsome bridge over the Wear was erected between 1772 and 1777, at the expense of the Dean and Chapter.

Durham is not distinguished for commerce or manufactures. Some years ago a woollen manufactory existed, which furnished employment for several hundred persons, but it has since been abandoned, and a cotton factory which had been established here was accidentally burnt down in January 1804, and has never been rebuilt.

DURHAM

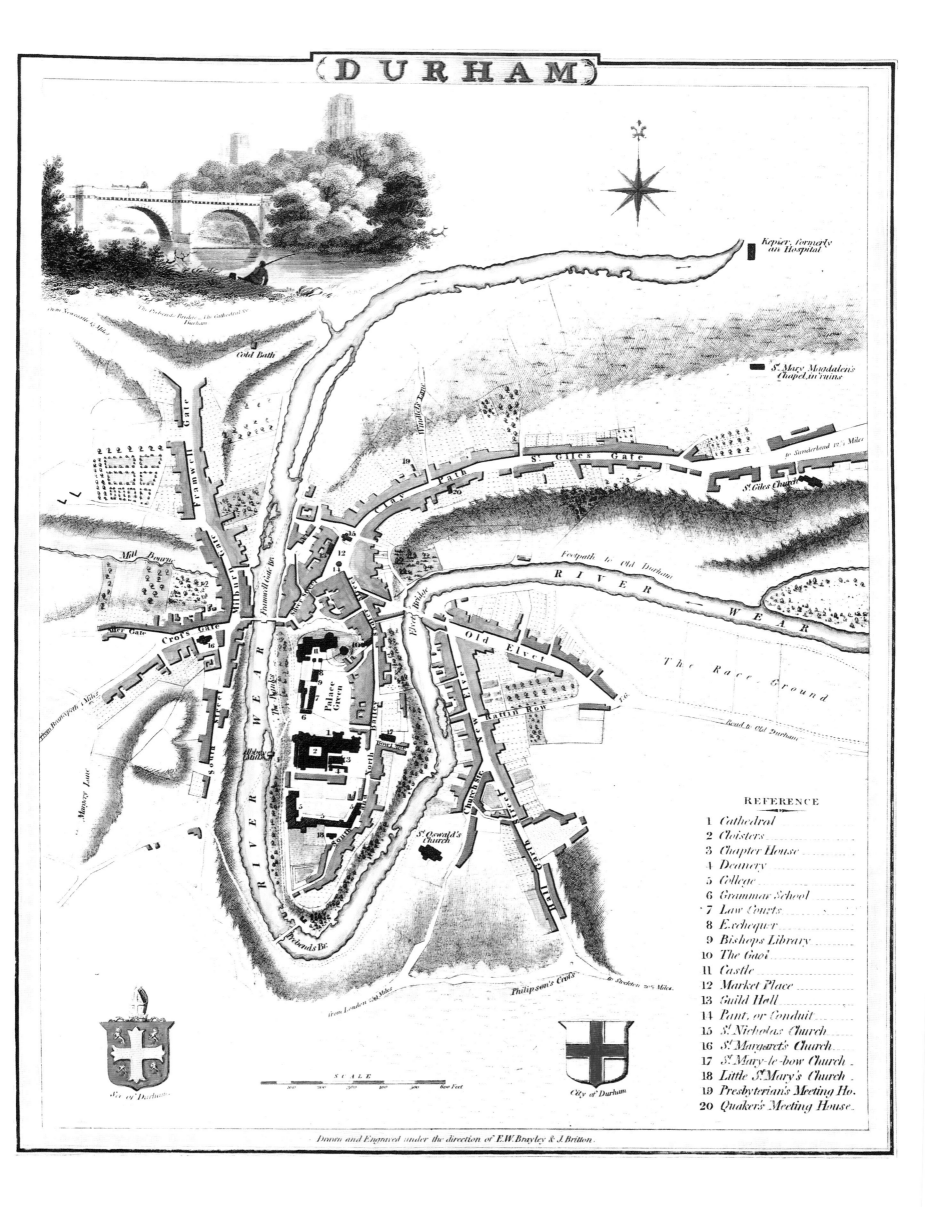

The Prebends Bridge & The Cathedral &c Durham

from Newcastle 15 Miles

Cold Bath

Kepier, formerly an Hospital

S.t Mary Magdalen's Chapel, in ruins

to Sunderland 12½ Miles

S.t Giles Gate

S.t Giles Church

Windmill Lane

Clay Path

Footpath to Old Durham

RIVER   WEAR

The Race-Ground

Road to Old Durham

Elvet Bridge

Old Elvet

Ratlin Row

Framwellgate Br.

Silver St.

Saddler St.

Gaol Bridge

New   Elvet

Church St.

Framwelgate

Hallgarth St.

Hallgarth

Milburn Gate

Mill Bourn

Nier Gate

Crofs Gate

St. Oswald's Church

Prebends Br.

Palace Green

The Banks

South   RIVER   WEAR

North Bailey

South Bailey

Bow Lane

Abbey House

Mavin's Lane

from Bishop's Auckland 5½ Miles

from London 258 Miles

Philipson's Crofs

to Stockton 20½ Miles

REFERENCE

1 Cathedral
2 Cloisters
3 Chapter House
4 Deanery
5 College
6 Grammar School
7 Law Courts
8 Exchequer
9 Bishops Library
10 The Gaol
11 Castle
12 Market Place
13 Guild Hall
14 Pant, or Conduit
15 S.t Nicholas Church
16 S.t Margaret's Church
17 S.t Mary-le-bow Church
18 Little S.t Mary's Church
19 Presbyterian's Meeting Ho.
20 Quaker's Meeting House

See of Durham

City of Durham

SCALE
100   200   300   400   500   600 Feet

Drawn and Engraved under the direction of E.W. Brayley & J. Britton.

Exeter

The county town of Devon, Exeter lies 171 miles from London, and has a population of 17,388.

An ancient city, the capital of Devonshire is situated on the eastern bank of the River Exe, about nine miles north of the English Channel.

This place was called by the Saxons 'Monkton' from the number of religious establishments it contained.

The ancient walls of the city included a space of ground four furlongs in length and three in breadth, and the area is intercepted by four principal streets, which meet near the centre, and diverging at right angles, connect the city with the suburbs. In 1769, the walls were standing, but many parts of them have since been taken down. The principal street, called High Street, has the appearance of antiquity, as have many of the buildings in different parts of the city; but within the last half century handsome edifices and new streets have been erected, some of which would not suffer from comparison with those in most other parts of the kingdom.

There is a handsome stone bridge over the Exe, erected some fifteen years since, at the expense of nearly £20,000.

In 1675, a canal was cut from Topsham to Exeter; the first canal carried out in the United Kingdom for the purpose of enabling sea-going vessels to pass to an inland port. By means of sluices and floodgates vessels of 150 tons burden are admitted to a good quay near the city walls.

The manufacture of coarse woollen goods has been carried on here very extensively, but it has much decayed of late years. Vast quantities of duroys and serges used to be exported to Spain, Portugal and the Mediterranean, to the estimated amount of £600,000 annually, but though these and other markets have failed, the demand for these articles is still considerable.

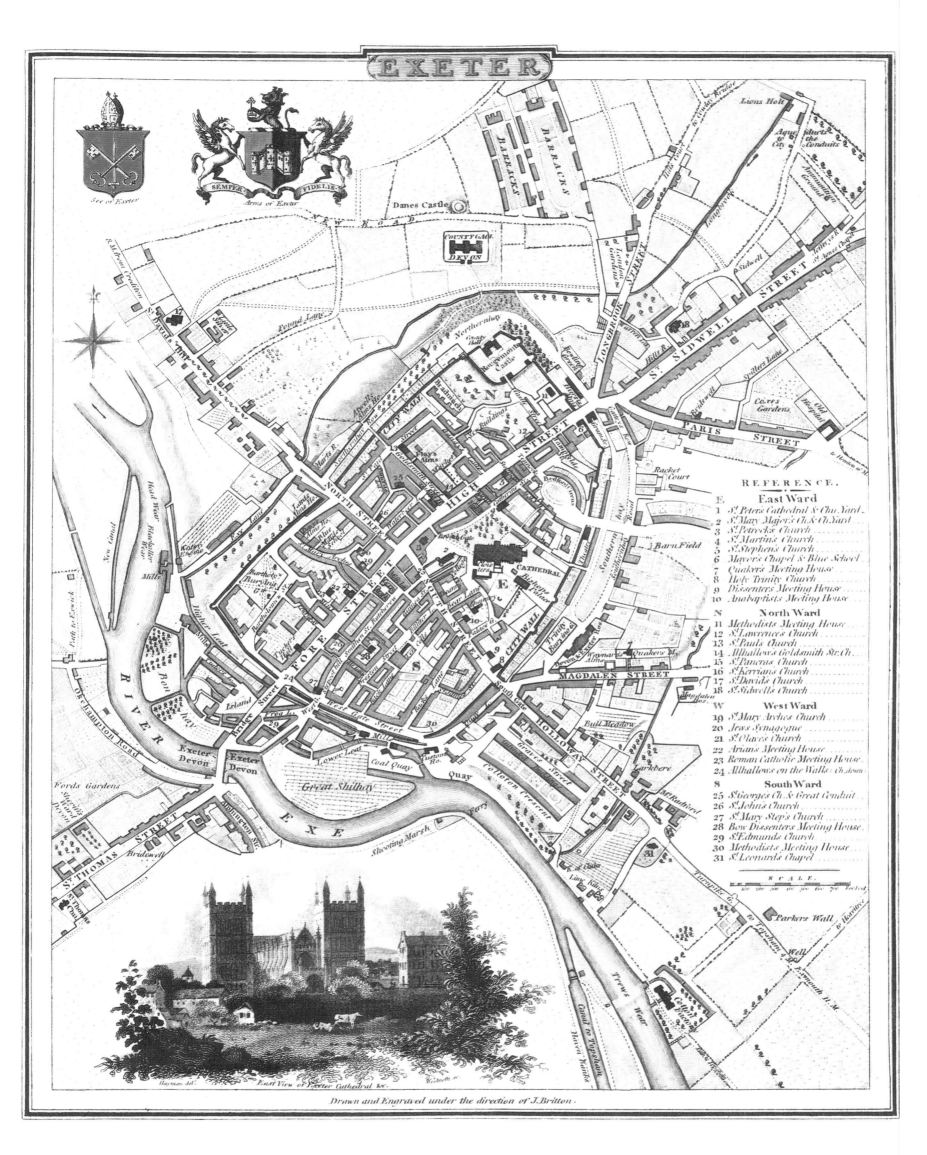

EXETER

REFERENCE.

East Ward

E.
1 St Peters Cathedral & Chu.Yard.
2 St Mary Majors Ch.& Ch.Yard.
3 St Petrocks Church
4 St Martins Church
5 St Stephens Church
6 Mayors Chapel & Blue School
7 Quakers Meeting House
8 Holy Trinity Church
9 Dissenters Meeting House
10 Anabaptists Meeting House

North Ward

N
11 Methodists Meeting House
12 St Lawrences Church
13 St Pauls Church
14 Allhallows Goldsmith Str.Ch.
15 St Pancras Church
16 St Kerrians Church
17 St Davids Church
18 St Sidwells Church

West Ward

W
19 St Mary Arches Church
20 Jews Synagogue
21 St Olaves Church
22 Arians Meeting House
23 Roman Catholic Meeting House
24 Allhallows on the Walls (Ch.down)

South Ward

S
25 St Georges Ch.& Great Conduit
26 St Johns Church
27 St Mary Steps Church
28 Bow Dissenters Meeting House
29 St Edmunds Church
30 Methodists Meeting House
31 St Leonards Chapel

SCALE.

See of Exeter

Arms of Exeter SEMPER FIDELIS.

Hayman del. East View of Exeter Cathedral &c. *W.Woolnoth sc.*

Drawn and Engraved under the direction of J.Britton.

Gloucester

Gloucester lies 104 miles from London, and has a population of 7,265. A city of high antiquity, the capital of the county to which it gives name, Gloucester stands in a plain on the eastern bank of the Severn. The choice of its site seems to have been decided by the increasing breadth of the river, this being the most southern point affording a safe and convenient transit to the western part of the county. Like many other places of Roman origin, Gloucester consists of four principal streets, diverging from a common centre; and it had anciently four gates which gave name to the streets which they respectively terminated, Eastgate, Southgate, Westgate and Northgate. The continuation of the eastern street is called Barton Street, in which a large fair is held annually in the month of September.

A quay with wharves for the loading and unloading of shipping extends along the banks of the Severn, from the county gaol towards the Westgate Bridge.

Ironworks formerly subsisted here, but these have long been discontinued, and cap-making, sugar-refining and glass-working which were once carried on very extensively have given place to other manufactures. Of these, pin-making was for a long time almost confined to this city, where the art was introduced in 1625 by John Tilsby. There is a bell-foundry in Oxbody Lane, which has been conducted for nearly one hundred and fifty years, during which period, between 3,000 and 4,000 bells have been cast, by members of a family named Ruddhall. A manufactory of shawls from fine English wool has been established in Northgate street; there is an iron-foundry in that part of the city called the Island; and there are also extensive brush manufactories and one, of some note, for making edge tools.

Two newspapers are published here, the *Gloucester Journal* and the *Gloucester Herald*, the former of which is one of the oldest and most respectable of the provincial journals.

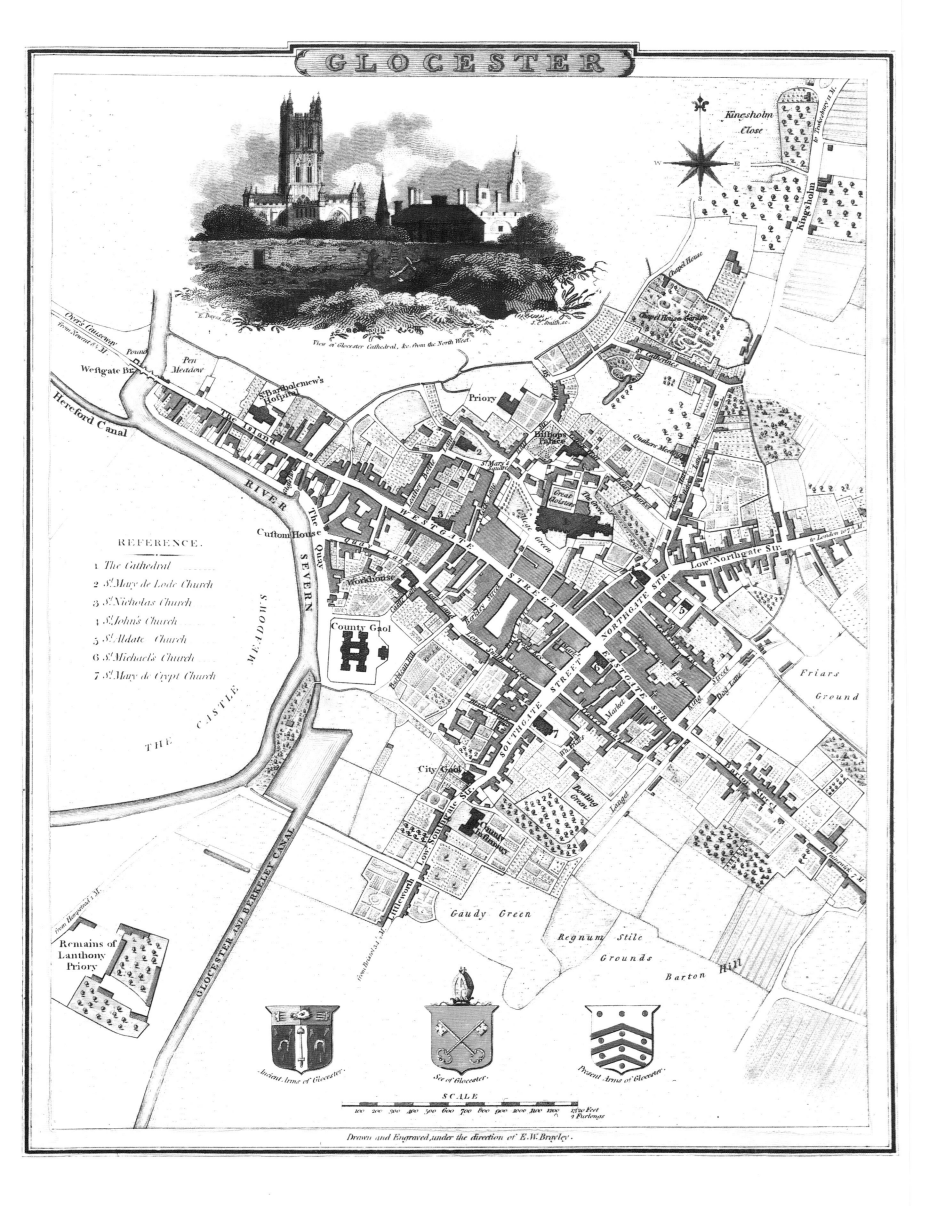

GLOCESTER

View of Glocester Cathedral, &c. from the North West.

E. Dayes, del.   J.C. Smith, sc.

Kingsholm Close

Kingsholm

to Tewksbury 11 M.

Chapel House

Chapel House Garden

Over's Causeway From Newent 8 M.

Pound

Westgate BR.

Pen Meadow

Hereford Canal

St. Bartholomew's Hospital

The Island

Priory

Bishops Palace

Quakers Meadow

RIVER SEVERN

The Quay

Custom House

Workhouse

St. Mary Square

Great Cloisters

The Grey

WESTGATE STREET

Black Green

to London 107½ M.

Low Northgate Str.

NORTHGATE STR.

THE CASTLE MEADOWS

County Gaol

Barbican Hill

EASTGATE STREET

SOUTHGATE STREET

Friars Ground

King Street

Dog Lane

City Gaol

Bowling Green

Longsmith Street

Market

County Infirmary

Barton Str.

Low Southgate Str.

from Hempstead 2 M.

GLOCESTER AND BERKELEY CANAL

Littleworth

from Bristol 34 ½ M.

Gaudy Green

Regnum Stile

Grounds

to Cheltenham 9 M.

Barton Hill

Remains of Lanthony Priory

REFERENCE.

1 The Cathedral
2 St. Mary de Lode Church
3 St. Nicholas Church
4 St. John's Church
5 St. Aldate Church
6 St. Michael's Church
7 St. Mary de Crypt Church

Ancient Arms of Glocester.

See of Glocester.

Present Arms of Glocester.

SCALE

100 200 300 400 500 600 700 800 900 1000 1100 1200 1300 Feet
2 Furlongs

Drawn and Engraved, under the direction of E.W. Brayley.

Hereford

Hereford lies 135 miles from London, with a population of 6,828. An ancient city, and the capital of the county. It stands nearly in the middle of the county, on low ground, and is bordered on the southern side by the River Wye. Hereford was capital of the ancient kingdom of Mercia, under the celebrated King Offa.

Hereford was anciently surrounded by a wall, with six gates, and fifteen watchtowers; but these as well as the castle have been entirely destroyed, and the keep having been levelled, no part of the walls is remaining; but the site of those which enclosed the larger ward is now converted into a public walk; which is deservedly admired. The city has several good streets which are broad and well paved, with many others of an inferior description. The buildings in general are handsome, and the vicinity of the city, especially near the banks of the Wye, is extremely pleasant.

The manufactures here are those of gloves, flannels and hats; several attempts have been made to introduce the woollen trade, but without success. Cider, hops and tanners' bark are the grand articles of commerce; and the Wye being navigable here for barges of considerable burden, coals and other articles are brought from the Forest of Dean. The want is greatly felt of a communication with Gloucester, such as would have been furnished by the Gloucester and Hereford Canal, which has been left unfinished.

Hereford is the birth-place of the famous Nell Gwynne, an actress, who became the mistress of Charles II.

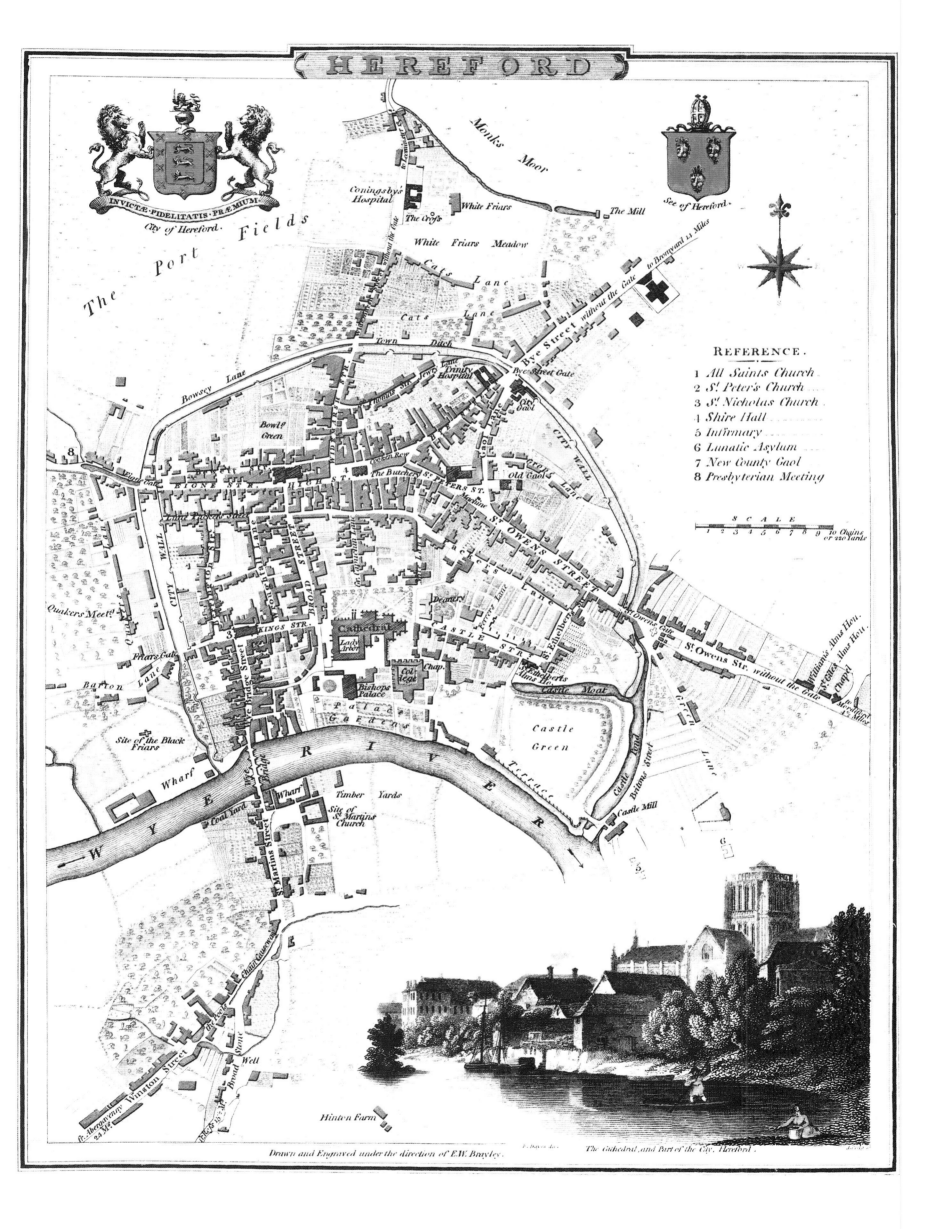

HEREFORD

INVICTÆ·FIDELITATIS·PRÆMIUM

City of Hereford.

See of Hereford.

REFERENCE.

1 *All Saints Church*
2 *St Peter's Church*
3 *St Nicholas Church*
4 *Shire Hall*
5 *Infirmary*
6 *Lunatic Asylum*
7 *New County Gaol*
8 *Presbyterian Meeting*

SCALE
1 2 3 4 5 6 7 8 9 10 Chains
or 220 Yards

Monk's Moor

Coningsbys Hospital
White Friars
The Cross
The Mill

White Friars Meadow

Cats Lane

The Port Fields

Cats Lane

Town Ditch

Bye Street without the Gate
to Bromyard 11 Miles

Bowsey Lane

Bye Street Gate

Trinity Hospital

Bowl.g Green

EIGNE STR.

HIGH ST.

Cooken Row

The Butchers Row

St PETERS ST.

Old Gaol

CITY WALL

Quakers Meet.g

KINGS STR.

BROAD STREET

Cathedral

Lady Arbor

Deanery

CASTLE STR.

St OWENS STREET

St Owens Gate

St Owens Str. without the Gate
to Ledbury 13 Miles

Friars Gate

Barton Lane

Site of the Black Friars

Col lege

Bishops Palace

Palace Garden

St Ethelberts Alms Ho.

St Ethelberts Alms Ho.

St Owens Str. without the Gate

St Williams Alms Hou.

St Giles Alms Hou.

Chapel

Wharf

Wharf

Coal Yard

Martins Street

Site of St Martins Church

Timber Yards

WYE RIVER

Castle Green

Castle Moat

Terrace

Castle Pond

Castle Mill

Britons Street

Green Lane

St Abergavenny Winston Street

Broad Stone

Well

Hinton Farm

Chain Causeway

Drawn and Engraved under the direction of E.W. Brayley.

The Cathedral, and Part of the City, Hereford.

Liverpool

Liverpool lies 204 miles from London, and in 1802 had a population of 77,653. The whole town with its proper suburbs includes an area of 4,000 yards from north to south, and 2,500 yards from east to west. The latter side is bounded by the River Mersey, and on the opposite side are the borders of the townships of West Derby, and Everton; whilst Toxteth Park skirts its southern side and the northern side joins the township of Kirkdale. The whole of this area however is not covered with buildings, though the practice of erecting new houses and forming new streets continues to prevail to an amazing extent; and, if persevered in, will in a short period occupy the whole space by a connected and spacious town. In 1774 the number of streets, lanes, alleys, &c. was 230; but this number has been greatly increased as the scheme of building several new streets at the south end of the town has been since that period in a degree carried into effect. The greatest disbursements occurred from 1786 to 1800, when Castle Street was widened, and other expensive improvements were made.

Among the number of commercial towns in Great Britain it may safely be said that not one has so rapidly advanced to as great extent, and as great opulence, as that of Liverpool. From a small inconsiderable hamlet, this thriving sea-port, by the spirited industry, enterprising pursuits, and speculating habits of its chief inhabitants, has, within the last century, been singularly advanced in the scale of national importance. A history of Liverpool must be an account of the people not the place; for if the town be divested of its complicated traffic, increased shipping, and nautical erections, it presents little else to recompense enquiry, or gratify curiosity.

The present prosperity of Liverpool has evidently arisen from a combination of causes; and among these may be chiefly noticed its natural situation, its free water carriage with the numerous manufacturing towns and mines of the county, and the enlightened policy of its civil government. As the Liverpool docks were the first reservoirs and harbours, for the accommodation of merchandise, ever constructed in this country, it will be necessary to detail some further particulars. The wet docks are five in number: the Old Dock, the Salthouse Dock, George's Dock, King's Dock, Queen's Dock. These, augmented by five graving docks, and three dry docks, presently occupy a space of about three miles in circumference.

In 1805, 4,618 ships with an aggregate tonnage of 464,482 tons were assessed for dock duties totalling £33,364 13s. 1d. Among the many and various articles of merchandise imported into the town in that year were 172,638 bags of cotton, 11,840 terces of coffee, 40,422 hogsheads of sugar, and 6,838 of tobacco, 5,285 logs of mahogany, and 5,708 elephants teeth.

Before the abolition of the slave trade it formed the grand source of commercial enterprise here, and it has been stated that nearly two-thirds of the population were interested in the traffic of human beings; but their wealth and industry are now devoted to purposes more adapted to the promotion of national prosperity.

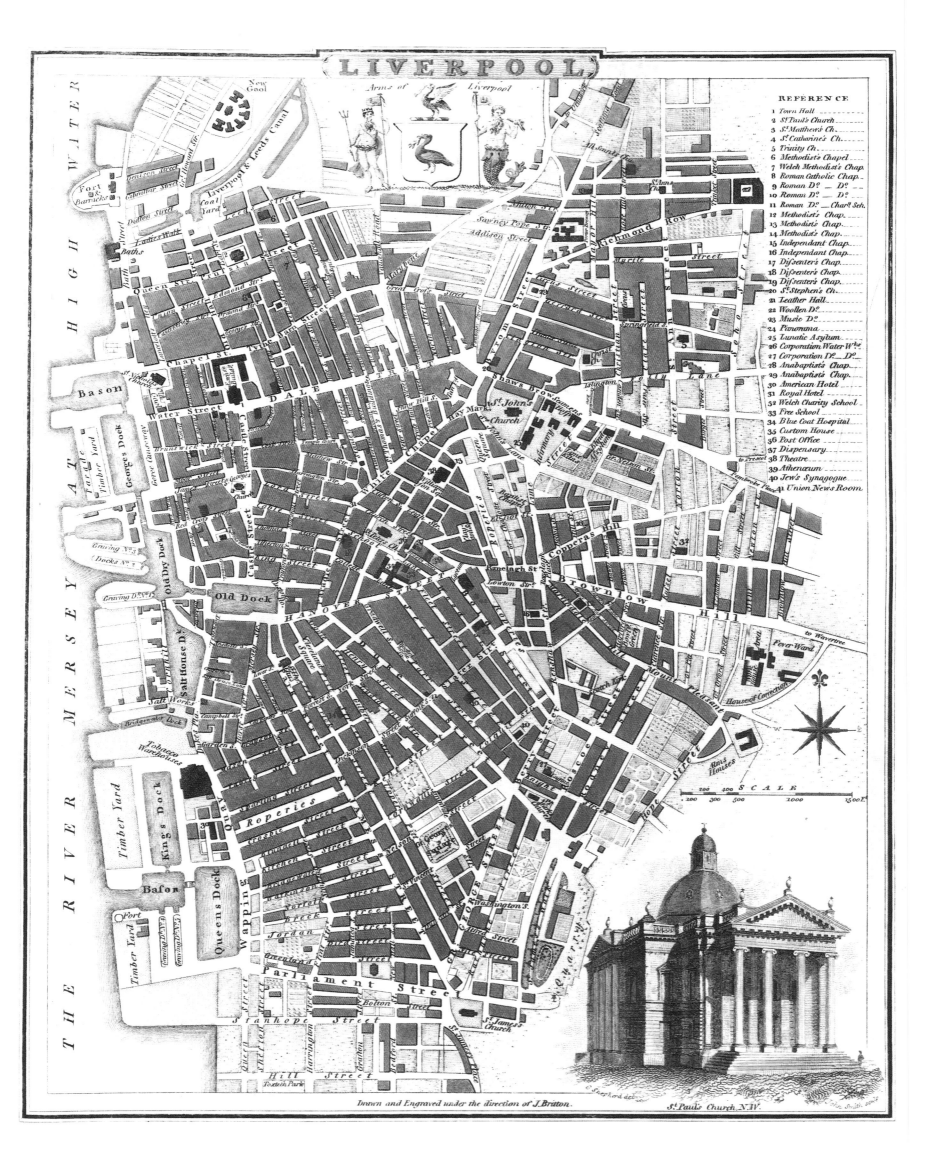

LIVERPOOL

Arms of Liverpool

THE RIVER MERSEY AT HIGH WATER

Fort & Barracks

New Gaol

Liverpool & Leeds Canal

Coal Yard

Bason

George's Dock

Timber Yard

Water Street

DALE

Old Dock

HANOVER STREET

Salt House D.

Salt Works

Tobacco Warehouses

Bridgewater Dock

Timber Yard

King's Dock

Queens Dock

Bason

Fort

Wapping

Roperies

Parliament Street

Stanhope Street

Hill Street

Toxteth Park

St John's Church

Shaws Brow

Richmond Row

Copperas Hill

BROWNLOW HILL

Fever Ward

House of Correction

Aim's Houses

to Wavertree

to Prescot

George St

George Square

Washington's

Street

St James's Church

Bolton Street

St Paul's Church. N.W.

SCALE
200 400
300 500 1000 1500 ft

Drawn and Engraved under the direction of J. Britton.

Manchester and Salford

Manchester lies 189 miles from London. The population of Manchester and Salford in 1801 was 84,020. The present Manchester is an immense manufacturing, mercantile, and trading town, consisting of a great number of streets, lanes, alleys, and courts, which are crowdedly filled with warehouses and factories. At the extremities of the town, however, are many comfortable and handsome houses, either standing alone or congregated in rows, places, and parades.

The manufactures of Manchester may be said to constitute the very soul of the place, and the factories its body. To furnish a full and satisfactory account of all the operations would require several volumes; which the nature of this work will not allow.

The high rank Manchester holds in the scale of commercial importance may be attributed to the nature and extent of the improvements introduced into the cotton-spinning trade.

The spinning concerns in the town and neighbourhood are numerous, and many of them of great magnitude, some employing from 30 to 70,000 spindles, and yielding upwards of 600,000 hanks per week, each hank measuring 840 yards, or in the whole 504,000,000 yards, a prodigious length to be the produce of six days' labour. Of the Lancashire spinners it may not be improper to mention here that more than 400 hanks have been drawn from four pounds of raw East India cotton, in total reaching upwards 180 miles, or nearly as far as from London to Manchester. Not more than half a century has elapsed since all the cotton yarn manufactured in this country was spun by hand; the successful application of mechanics to this branch of business means that what would, thirty years since, have required some 600 women or girls to have performed, can now be done by one man and four children!

'The rapid increase in the number of spinning engines, which took place in consequence of the expiration of Arkwright's patent, forms a new era not only in manufactures and commerce, but also in the dress of both sexes. Women of all ranks are clothed in British manufactures of cotton from the muslin cap on the crown of the head to the cotton stocking under the sole of the foot' (MacPherson's *Annals of Commerce*).

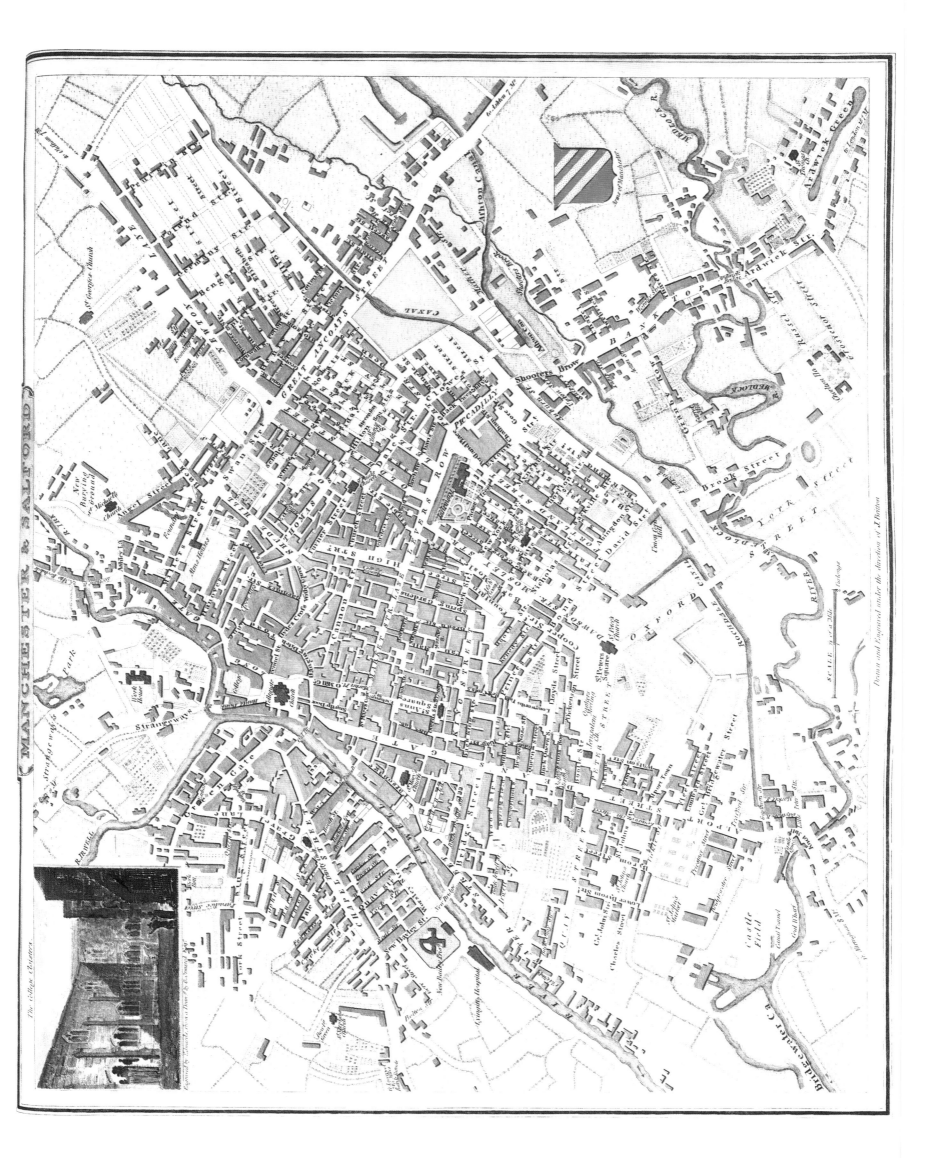

MANCHESTER & SALFORD

Newcastle upon Tyne and Gateshead

Newcastle lies 301 miles from London, and has a population of 27,587 (1811). The town occupies the north bank of the River Tyne over which there is a handsome stone bridge, connecting this place with Gateshead, in the county of Durham. The town, including those parts without the walls, extends about two miles along the banks of the Tyne, and one mile from the river-side towards the north and north-west; the ground being uneven but rising as it recedes from the river. The streets near the Tyne, which are the most ancient, are narrow, steep, and irregular. The buildings on the declivity of the hill are extremely crowded.

The bridge over the Tyne was erected in the place of a former bridge destroyed by the great inundation in November, 1771. It extends six hundred feet, consisting of nine elliptical arches, strongly constructed of stone, at a cost of more than £30,000, and completed in 1781.

The importance and prosperity of Newcastle have chiefly originated from the coal-trade, for the prosecution of which the town is admirably situated on the bank of a navigable river, and in the midst of one of the most extensive coalfields in Great Britain. The trade in coal between Newcastle and London was authorized by government in 1381. By 1699, two-thirds of the coal trade of this kingdom belonged to this town, whence 300,000 chaldrons a year were sent to the metropolis. In 1811, the quantity of coal shipped from Newcastle was 634,371 chaldrons sent coast-wise and 18,054 overseas. Newcastle carries on trade with the south of Europe, whence are imported wines and fruits, with Norway and the Baltic for corn, iron, timber, hemp, and other commodities; and about three ships are sent annually from this port to the Greenland fisheries. The principal exports from the River Tyne, besides coal, are lead, grindstones, salt, butter, tallow, and salmon, and a variety of manufactured articles.

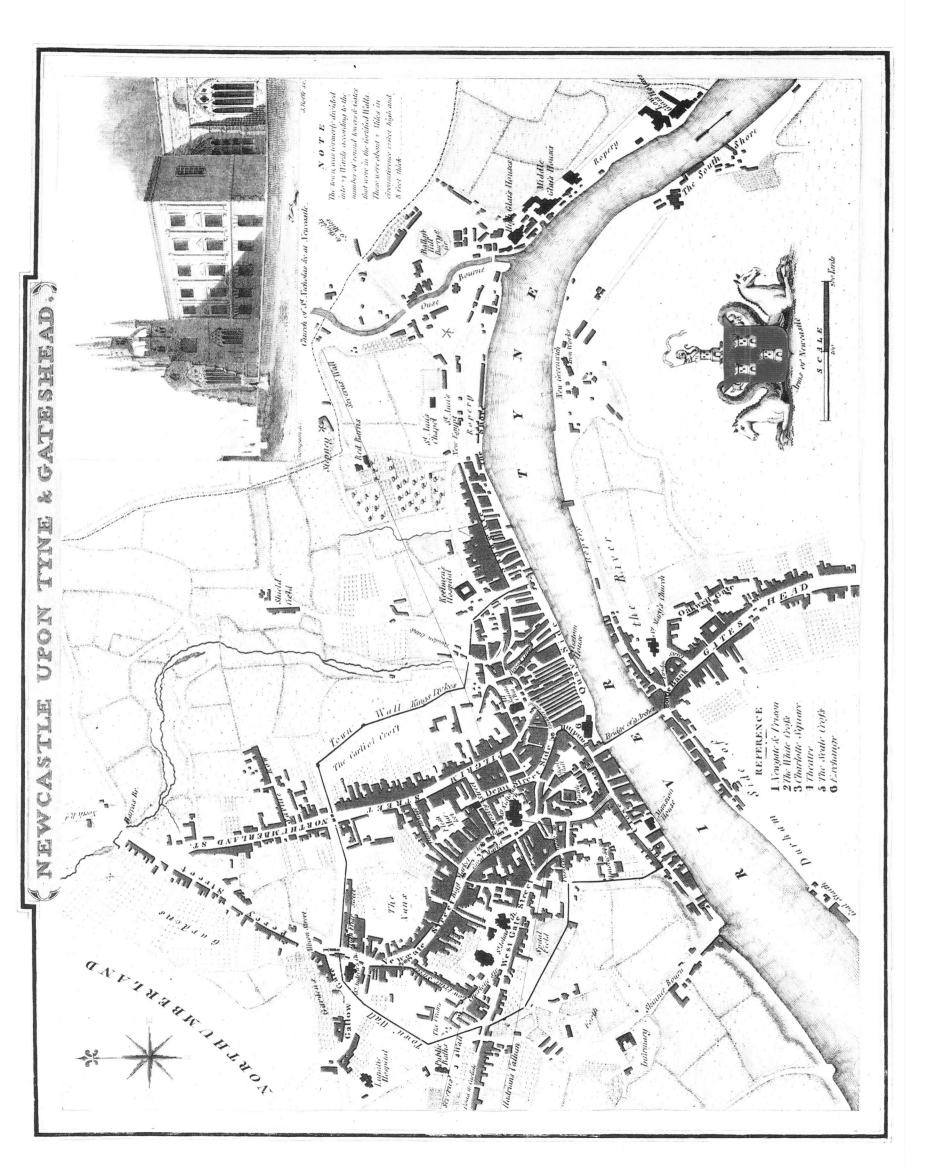

NEWCASTLE UPON TYNE & GATESHEAD.

Northampton

Northampton lies 66 miles from London, and has a population of 7,020. The county town of Northampton is situated on an eminence on the northern bank of the River Nene, near the centre of the county, at the junction of several roads from the northern to the southern and western parts of England.

On the 20th of September, 1675, the town suffered from a dreadful fire which destroyed buildings and other property amounting in value to £150,000, and deprived 700 families of their habitations. An Act of Parliament was speedily procured to regulate the rebuilding of the town; the King gave 1,000 tons of timber from the royal forests for the new buildings; and the damage occasioned by this disaster was in no long time entirely repaired.

The finest street in the town is that called The Drapery, remarkable for its width and handsome buildings; and at its eastern extremity is The Woodhill, a noble square, said to be one of the handsomest market-places in Europe. The streets in general display regularity of arrangement, and most of the houses and other buildings are constructed of a kind of stone somewhat of a red colour.

Northampton is noted for the manufacture of boots and shoes, which is carried on upon a very extensive scale; currying and dressing of leather, lace-making, and the manufacture of brass and iron-work are also largely prosecuted here. A considerable share of trade, likewise, arises from the constant passage of travellers by stage-coaches from London to Liverpool, Manchester &c.

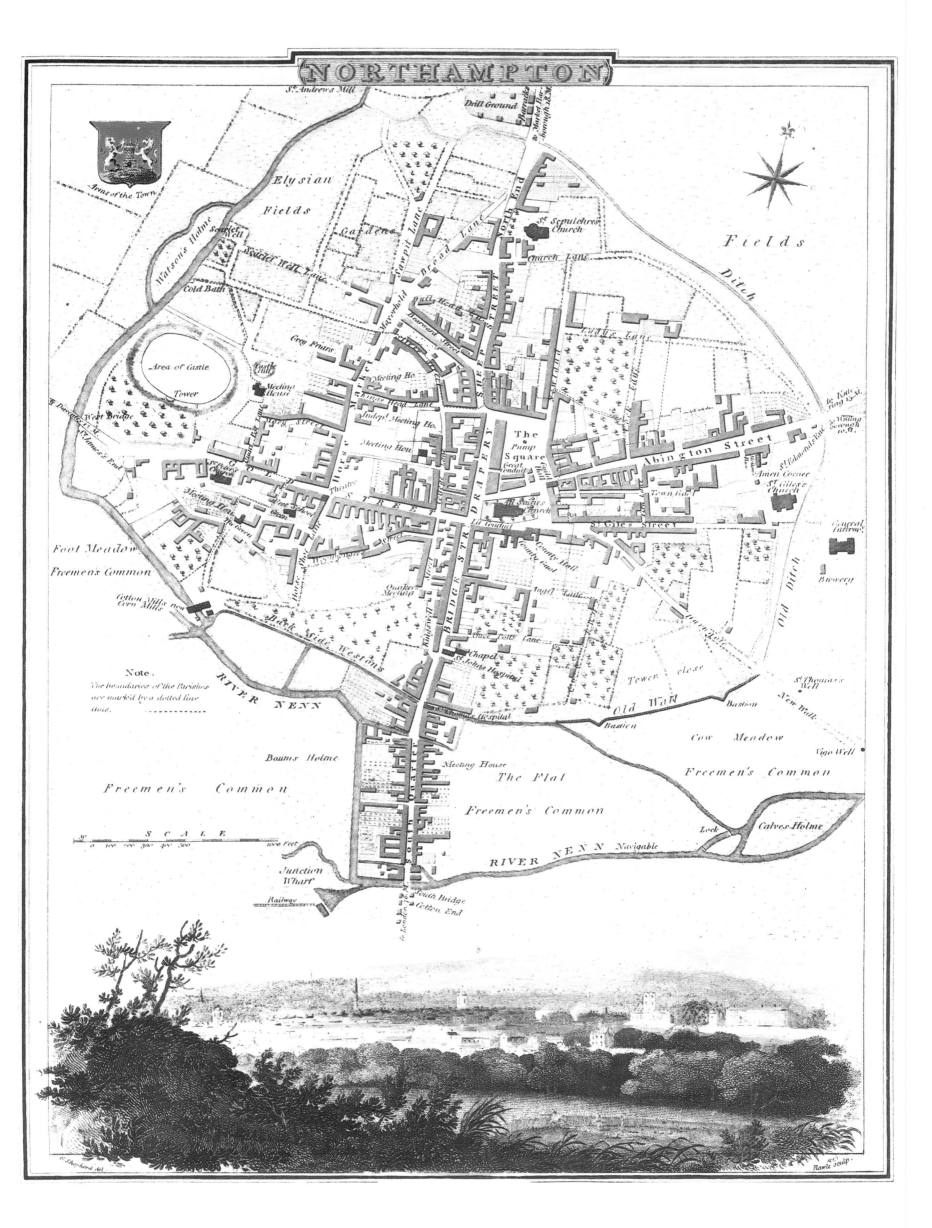

NORTHAMPTON

Arms of the Town

St. Andrews Mill

Drill Ground

Barracks

to Market Harborough 13 M.

Elysian Fields

Watsons Holme

Scarlet Well

Bridle Well Lane

Cold Bath

Garden

Sawpit Lane

Broad Lane

North End

St. Sepulchres Church

Church Lane

Fields

Ditch

Grey Friars

Mayorhold

Bull Head

Bearward Street

Sheep Street

Castle Lane

Area of Castle

Castle Hill

Tower

Meeting House

Meeting Ho.

Kings Head Lane

Indepl. Meeting Ho.

Grey Friars

The Pump Square

Great Conduit

Gold Street

to Kettering 13 M.

to Welling borough 10 M.

W. Dayclifee St.W.

West Bridge

St. Peters Church

Thames End

Horse Street

Meeting House

Theatre

Gold Street

Bridge Street

Drapery

St. Saviors Church

Abington Street

to St. Edmonds End

Amen Corner

St. Giles Church

Meeting House

Free School

The Green

Westminster

The Green

Lit. Conduit

County Court

County Hall

Town Hall

St. Giles Street

General Infirmary

Brewery

Foot Meadow

Freemen's Common

Cotton Mills now Corn Mills

Back Side Westons

Quakers Meeting

Kingswell

Three Potts Lane

Angel Lane

Chapel Lane

Tower close

Old Wall

St. Thomas's Well

New Walk

Note.
The boundaries of the Parishes are marked by a dotted line thus. - - - - - - -

RIVER NENN

Chapel

St. Johns Hospital

St. Thomas Hospital

Bastion

Bastion

Cow Meadow

Vigo Well

Baums Holme

Meeting House

The Flat

Freemen's Common

Freemen's Common

Freemen's Common

SCALE
0 100 200 300 400 500   1000 Feet

Junction Wharf

Railway

to London Road

South Bridge

Cotton End

RIVER NENN Navigable

Lock

Calves Holme

G. Shepherd del.

Rawle sculp.

Norwich

Norwich lies 108 miles from London, and has a population of 36,854. The city of Norwich, metropolis of the county of Norfolk is situated principally on the declivity of a hill on the north side of the navigable River Wensum, over which there are six bridges.

The city is about a mile and a half in length and about a mile and a quarter in breadth; and the houses being generally furnished with gardens, it occupies more ground in proportion to its population than any other city in England, which has given rise to its appellation 'a city in an orchard'. It was anciently encompassed by a wall with forty strong towers of which there are some remains still visible.

Among the public buildings, one of the most important is the castle, which stands on the summit of a vast mount, artificially constructed, in the middle of the city. The castle precinct includes somewhat more than six acres of ground which, though surrounded by the city, belongs to the county of Norfolk.

The city of Norwich has long been famous for its woollen, worsted, and silk manufactures, which in 1724 afforded employment for about 120,000 persons, many of whom, however, resided in the surrounding country. The chief articles made here are bombazines, crapes, camlets, and other fabrics composed of silk and worsted; shawls, damasks, some cotton and woollen goods, and a variety of fancy pieces. The bombazine manufacture has considerably declined, and to a certain extent, has been superseded by that of silk goods, for which the abundance of machinery and artisans affords every facility. Here are extensive iron and brass foundries, breweries, snuff mills, vinegar works on a very extensive scale, oil and mustard mills, and corn mills. The products of these and other manufactories are exported to Holland, Ostend, Hamburg, the Baltic, Russia, Spain, Portugal, Italy, the East and West Indies, and North and South America.

Norwich has of late years been greatly improved partly in consequence of an Act of Parliament, obtained in 1806, appointing commissioners for paving the streets.

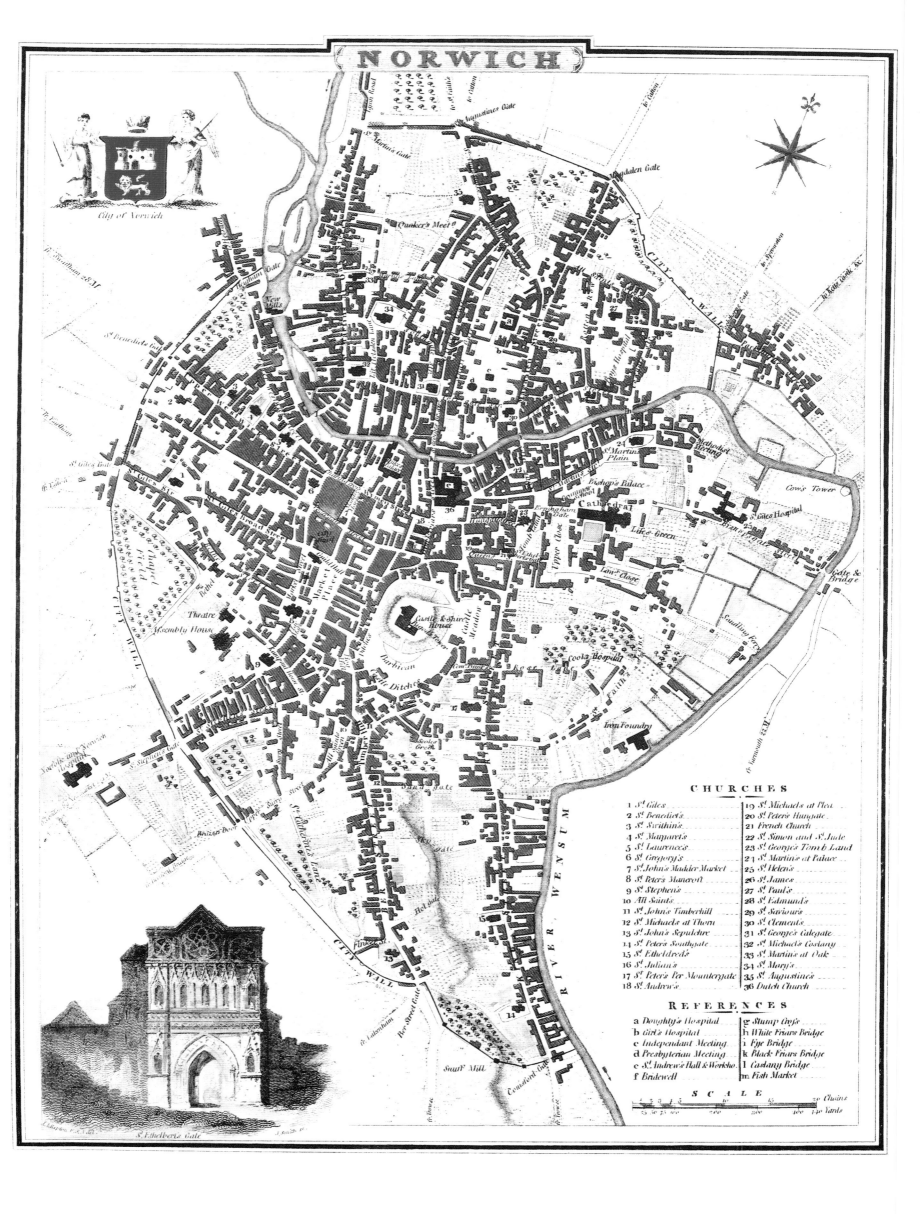

NORWICH

City of Norwich

S.t Ethelbert's Gate

CHURCHES

1 S.t Giles
2 S.t Benedict's
3 S.t Swithin's
4 S.t Margaret's
5 S.t Laurence's
6 S.t Gregory's
7 S.t John's Madder Market
8 S.t Peter's Mancroft
9 S.t Stephen's
10 All Saints
11 S.t John's Timberhill
12 S.t Michael's at Thorn
13 S.t John's Sepulchre
14 S.t Peter's Southgate
15 S.t Etheldred's
16 S.t Julian's
17 S.t Peter's Per Mountergate
18 S.t Andrew's

19 S.t Michael's at Plea
20 S.t Peter's Hungate
21 French Church
22 S.t Simon and S.t Jude
23 S.t George's Tomb Land
24 S.t Martin's at Palace
25 S.t Helen's
26 S.t James
27 S.t Paul's
28 S.t Edmund's
29 S.t Saviour's
30 S.t Clement's
31 S.t George's Colegate
32 S.t Michael's Costany
33 S.t Martin's at Oak
34 S.t Mary's
35 S.t Augustine's
36 Dutch Church

REFERENCES

a Doughty's Hospital
b Girl's Hospital
c Independant Meeting
d Presbyterian Meeting
e S.t Andrew's Hall & Worksho.
f Bridewell

g Stump Cross
h White Friars Bridge
i Fye Bridge
k Black Friars Bridge
l Costany Bridge
m Fish Market

SCALE

Oxford

Oxford lies 54 miles from London, with a population of 11,694. Pleasantly situated on a gentle eminence, in the midst of fertile meadows, at the confluence of the River Cherwell with the Thames.

The city, together with its suburbs, comprises an area of about three miles in circumference, extending a mile and a quarter from east to west, and nearly as far from north to south. The city itself is of an oval figure, and was formely surrounded by a wall, with bastions, one hundred and fifty feet distant from each other; but of these works there are few traces remaining. Three of the four principal entrances to this city are over bridges. From Magdalen Bridge the High Street, which has been accounted one of the noblest streets in Europe, stretches westward through the whole city. At Carfax, the 'four ways', this grand avenue is crossed by St Giles', the other principal street, and from these most of the other streets diverge in several directions. The High Street is remarkable, not only for its length, but for the graceful curvature that it exhibits, and the number of public buildings by the fronts of which it is ornamented. On the north side of the High Street there is a commodious market place, the entrances to which are secured by iron gates, and the houses in front of it are fitted up as shops.

Oxford enjoys a considerable share of commerce, through the transit of various articles, chiefly corn and coal, by means of the Thames and Oxford Canal. Brawn, for which this place has long been noted, is made in considerable quantities, both for immediate consumption and for the London market.

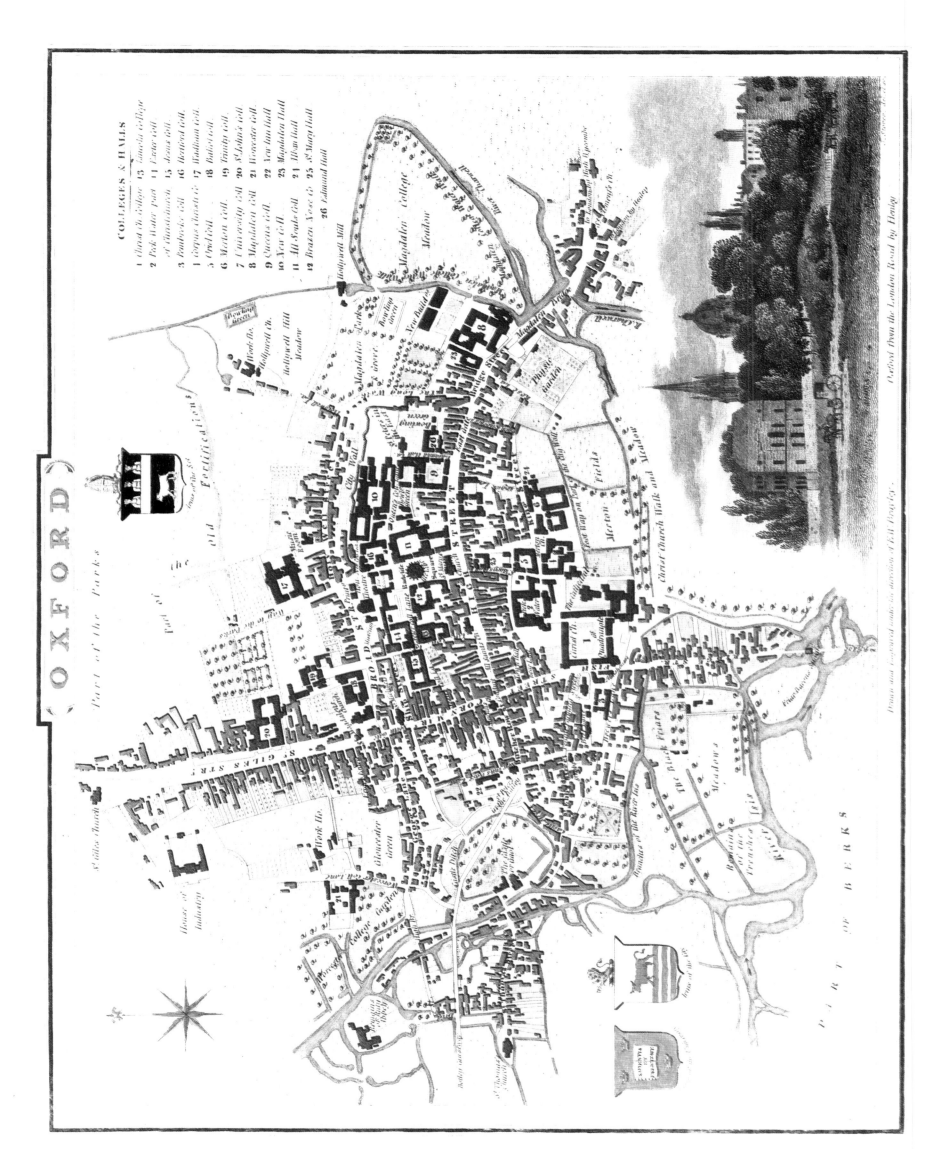

OXFORD

COLLEGES & HALLS

1 Christ Church College
2 Pek Water part of Christchurch
3 Peubrooks Cell
4 Corpus Christi C.
5 Oriel Cell
6 Merton Cell
7 University Cell
8 Magdalen Cell
9 Queens Cell
10 New Cell
11 All Souls Cell
12 Brazen Nose C.
13 Lincoln College
14 Exeter Cell
15 Jesus Cell
16 Trinitit Cell
17 Wadham Cell
18 Baliol Cell
19 Trinity Cell
20 St Johns Cell
21 Worcester Cell
22 New Inn Hall
23 Magdalen Hall
24 Hart Hall
25 St Mary Hall
26 Edmund Hall

Oxford from the London Road by Henley

St Albans

St Albans lies 21 miles from London, and has a population of 3,038. A borough and market town, situated on the summit and northern declivity of a hill, skirted by the rivulet Ver, near the vestiges of the ancient town of Verulam and the line of the Roman Watling Street.

The town had its origin in the abbey founded in 795 by Offa, King of Mercia. The abbey church, which claims particular attention for its size, beauty, and antiquity, is constructed of Roman brick. The tombs of the founder, Offa, and Humphrey, Duke of Gloucester are shewn here. The other edifices in this borough are no way remarkable; the principal are the Town Hall and Market House. St Albans consists principally of three streets. The market is well supplied with wheat. There is a free grammar school, and alms houses for 36 decayed men and women.

Little remains of the ancient Verulam, but a small part of its wall and some earthworks; but the Roman antiquities discovered on the site from time to time have been very numerous.

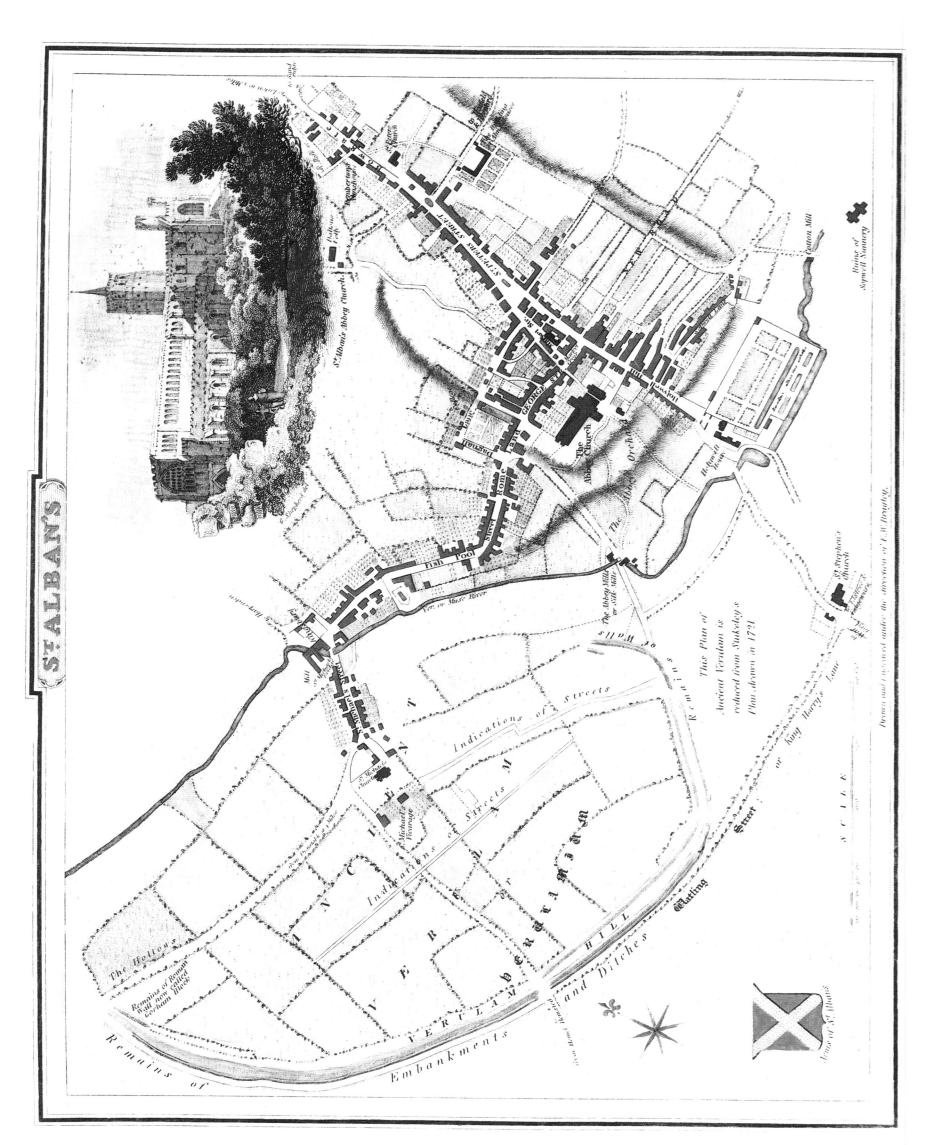

St ALBAN'S

Ruins of
Sopwell Nunnery

Cotton Mill

St Albans Abbey Church

The Abbey Church

St Peters Church

St Michaels Church

St Stephens Church

The Abbey Mills
or Silk Mills

Ver or Muse River

Fish Pool

Remains of Roman
Wall now called
Gorham Block

The Hollows

A N C I E N T   V E R U L A M I U M

Indications of Streets

Indications of Streets

Remains of

Embankments

Watling Street; or King Harry's Lane

and Ditches

VERULAM HILL

This Plan of
Ancient Verulam is
reduced from Stukeley's
Plan, drawn in 1721

Drawn and Engraved under the direction of E. W. Brayley.

SCALE

Arms of St Albans

Winchester

Winchester lies 62 miles from London, and has a population of 6,171. An ancient city, it occupies the eastern declivity of an eminence, at the base of which flows the River Itchen. The city consists of a spacious street, extending about half a mile from north to south, intersected at right angles by several smaller streets, of nearly an equal length. The buildings chiefly occupy the area within the ancient walls, which were built of flint. There were anciently four gates, but the west gate alone is now remaining, the others have been taken down, in consequence of an Act of Parliament for the improvement of the city, passed in 1770. The trade of this city is quite inconsiderable, and the manufactures are almost all of a local description.

The city appears to have been founded at a period of remote antiquity, and was called by the Britons, Caer Gwent, or the White City, from its being built on a chalky soil. Though London has long since superseded it as the metropolis of the kingdom, a memorial of its ancient superiority remains in the national denomination of measures of quantity, as Winchester ells and Winchester quarts, the use of which has but recently been replaced by imperial measures.

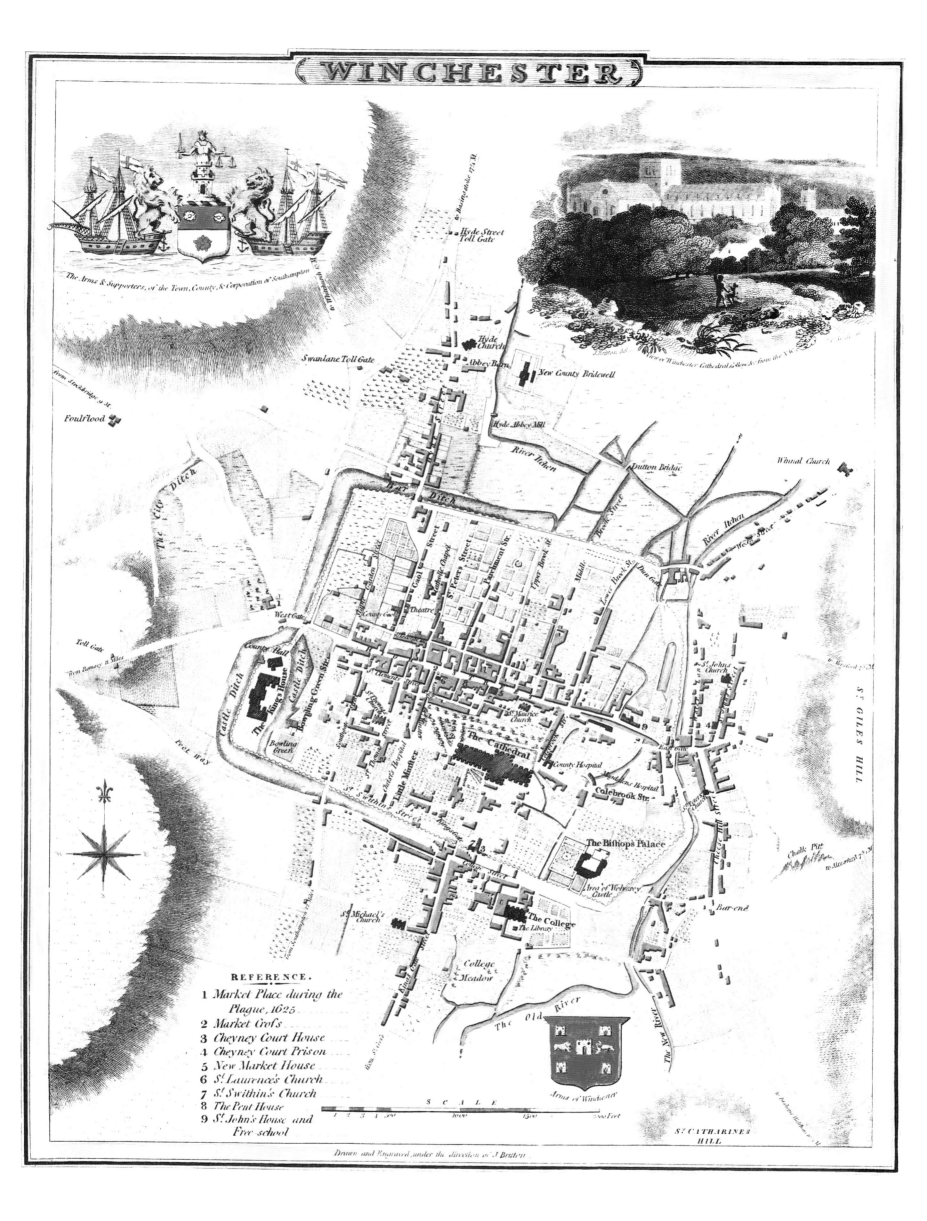

WINCHESTER

The Arms & Supporters, of the Town, County, & Corporation of Southampton.

View of Winchester Cathedral Colleges &c. from the N.W.

REFERENCE.
1 Market Place during the
    Plague, 1625
2 Market Cross
3 Cheyney Court House
4 Cheyney Court Prison
5 New Market House
6 St Laurence's Church
7 St Swithin's Church
8 The Pent House
9 St John's House and
    Free school

SCALE

Arms of Winchester

Drawn and Engraved, under the direction of J. Britton.

Worcester

Worcester lies 111 miles from London, with a population of 15,212. This city is agreeably situated, on rising ground, on the eastern bank of the Severn, over which there is a stone bridge of five arches, erected in 1780. The Foregate Street is a long and spacious avenue of well-built houses, terminated at one end by the church of St Nicholas. The market place in the High Street is a spacious area, with an ornamental arched entrance, the buildings of which were erected in 1804.

The quantity of fruit sold at this market in the proper season is astonishing: two and even three tons of cherries have been sold on a Saturday morning before 5 o'clock.

Worcester was formerly distinguished for the manufacture of woollen goods, now extinct. At present it is much noted for porcelain or chinaware, and gloves, especially the former.

The manufacture of porcelain was introduced here about 1751, conducted in two very extensive establishments, the one by Messrs Flight, Barr and Flight, and called the Royal China Manufactory, being under the patronage of their Majesties, and the other Messrs Chamberlain and Co., under the patronage of His Royal Highness, the Prince Regent.

The glove manufactory is also deserving of notice, as it is conducted on a very extensive scale, those of Worcester and its vicinity being much admired. This trade is carried on by 70 masters, who give employment to about 6,000 individuals, principally females. Among the other manufactures may be mentioned those of lace, iron, distilled spirits, nails, tanned leather, and turnery ware. In the markets take place large sales of corn and hops, the corn-market being held at the east end of Silver Street, and the hop-market, in an area at the south end of Foregate Street, where warehouses and offices have been erected.

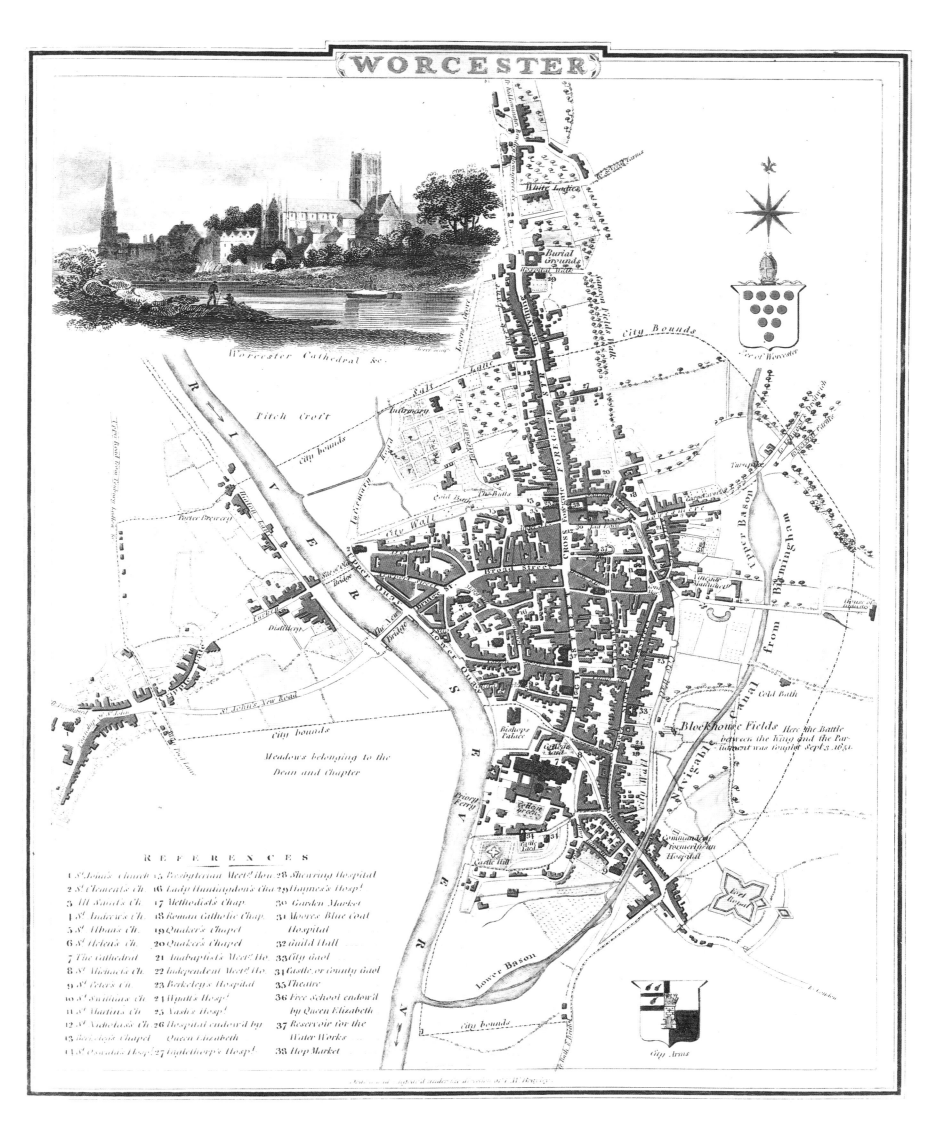

WORCESTER

Worcester Cathedral &c.

See of Worcester

White Ladies

Burial Grounds

City Bounds

Pitch Croft

Infirmary

City bounds

Porter Brewery

City Wall

The Butts

Cross

Distillery

The New Bridge

St Johns New Road

City bounds

Meadows belonging to the
Dean and Chapter

Broad Street

Bishops Palace

College Green

Blockhouse Fields *Here the Battle
between the King and the Parliament was fought Sept 3. 1651*

Cold Bath

Priory Ferry

Castle Hill

Commandery formerly an
Hospital

Fort Royal

Lower Bason

City bounds

City Arms

REFERENCES

1 St Johns Church	15 Presbyterian Meet Hou	28 Shearing Hospital
2 St Clements Ch.	16 Lady Huntingdon's Cha	29 Haynes's Hosp.l
3 All Saints Ch.	17 Methodists Chap	30 Garden Market
4 St Andrew's Ch.	18 Roman Catholic Chap.	31 Moores Blue Coat
5 St Albans Ch.	19 Quaker's Chapel	Hospital
6 St Helen's Ch.	20 Quaker's Chapel	32 Guild Hall
7 The Cathedral	21 Anabaptist's Meet Ho.	33 City Gaol
8 St Michael's Ch.	22 Independent Meet Ho.	34 Castle, or County Gaol
9 St Peters Ch.	23 Berkeley's Hospital	35 Theatre
10 St Swithins Ch	24 Wyatt's Hosp.l	36 Free School endow'd
11 St Martin's Ch	25 Nash's Hosp.l	by Queen Elizabeth
12 St Nicholas's Ch	26 Hospital endow'd by	37 Reservoir for the
13 Berkeley's Chapel	Queen Elizabeth	Water Works
14 St Oswald's Hosp.l	27 Inglethorpe's Hosp.l	38 Hop Market

GEORGE LOADER

Chichester

Plan of the City of Chichester, from an Actual Survey taken April 1812. George Loader, Surveyor.

From: James Dalaway, *The History of the Western Division of the County of Sussex . . .*, 1815. Copper engraving, 327 × 242mm

Chichester is 62 miles from London; the population in 1831 was 7,362. The city is situated on a gentle eminence, surrounded on all sides, except the north, by the small River Lavant. The modern town consists of four principal streets which meet in a common centre, and are called after the cardinal points of the compass. Each of these streets was formerly closed by a gate, and the whole is still surrounded by a wall, supposed to have been erected by the Romans. At the intersection of the four streets is a cross of an octagonal form supported on eight arches. The Guildhall is a spacious ancient building, but obscurely situated. Over the market-house, which is a neat and elegant structure, is the council chamber; and adjoining is a subscription assembly room. The cathedral is by far the most conspicuous edifice in the city. It was erected in the twelfth century, in the form of a cross, and is an exceedingly handsome structure. The bishop's palace, which was erected in 1727, possesses very handsome and extensive gardens.

The trade of Chichester is not extensive, though situated near an arm of the sea, owing to the difficulty of entering the harbour, except at spring tides. Here was anciently an extensive manufactory of needles, which is now wholly extinct; but the woollen manufacture is partially cultivated and at Itchelson much salt is made. On every other Wednesday is a market for the sale of sheep and black cattle, the most extensive of the county, great quantities being purchased both for Portsmouth and London.

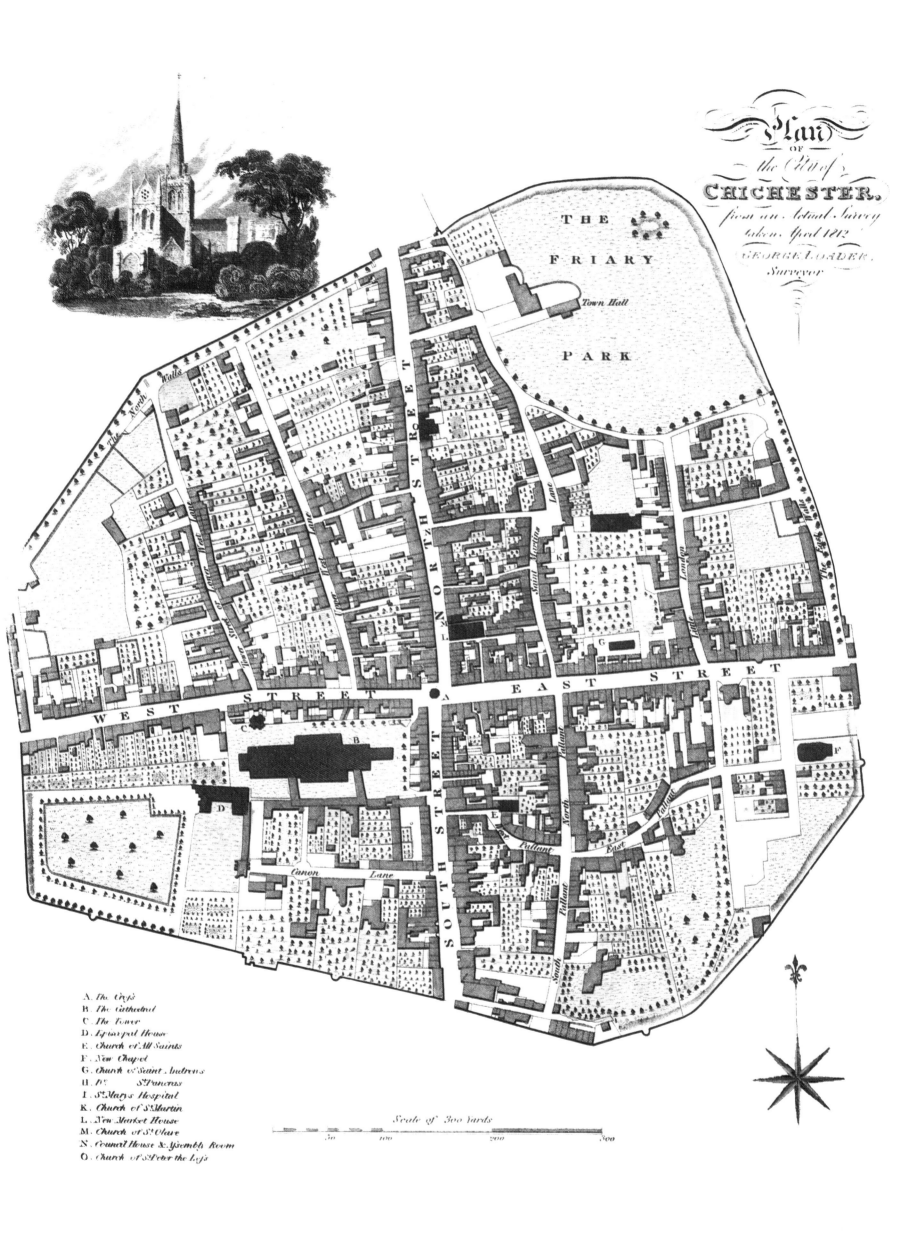

Plan
OF
the City of
CHICHESTER.
from an Actual Survey
taken April 1812
GEORGE LOADER,
Surveyor.

THE
FRIARY

PARK

Town Hall

NORTH STREET

WEST STREET

EAST STREET

SOUTH STREET

Canon Lane

Saint Martins Lane

North Pallant

East Pallant

South Pallant

West Pallant

North Walls

A. The Cross
B. The Cathedral
C. The Tower
D. Episcopal House
E. Church of All Saints
F. New Chapel
G. Church of Saint Andrews
H. D.º St Pancras
I. St Marys Hospital
K. Church of St Martin
L. New Market House
M. Church of St Olave
N. Council House & Assembly Room
O. Church of St Peter the less

Scale of 300 Yards

50   100   200   300

Tunbridge Wells

Map of Tunbridge Wells, in the county of Kent. shewing the Situation of The New Church. and the contiguous proposed Improvements, on the Calverley Estate. as Designed by Decimus Burton. 1828.

Separate publication, engraved by James and Josiah Neele for S. Rhodes, and published in London in 1828.
Engraving, 515 × 565mm.

Tunbridge Wells is located 36 miles from London, and its population in 1836 was 8,302. A large and populous hamlet, which has long been known and frequented as a watering-place on account of its mineral spring which was discovered in 1606.

In the reign of Charles II, the present divisions of the place appear to have been established with the appellations which they still retain. Mount Sion was the adopted seat of the Presbyterians and the Independents on which hill they had their respective meeting houses; while Mount Ephraim was the station of the Baptists.

Towards the end of the seventeenth century the walks and assembly rooms were arranged according to their present form. By an Act of Parliament in 1740, it was made 'illegal to erect any buildings on the common or . . . to build on any spot where a building had not previously existed' to which stipulation, Tunbridge Wells owes much of its present attraction.

There are three principal groups of buildings. That part called the Wells is situated at the point of junction of the three parishes, Tunbridge, Speldhurst and Frant; and here are the spa, the public baths, the chapel and also numerous shops and a market place. Mount Sion, adjoining the Wells on the north east is chiefly occupied by lodging houses, agreeably shaded by trees. Mount Ephraim, about half a mile north-westward of the Parade, was once the most fashionable quarter, but the buildings now consist principally of private mansions and lodging houses. Among the numerous improvements carrying on, the New Park on the Calverley Estate will be very striking, being studded with handsome stone-built villas of the first class. The well, or spring, is situated in a sandy valley, encompassed by hills; the water owes its virtues to the iron it contains. It is reckoned efficacious in cases of dyspepsia, nervous affections and other diseases attended with debility.

The New Church has been recently erected by Mr Decimus Burton, in the pointed style of architecture, at the expense of about £12,000.

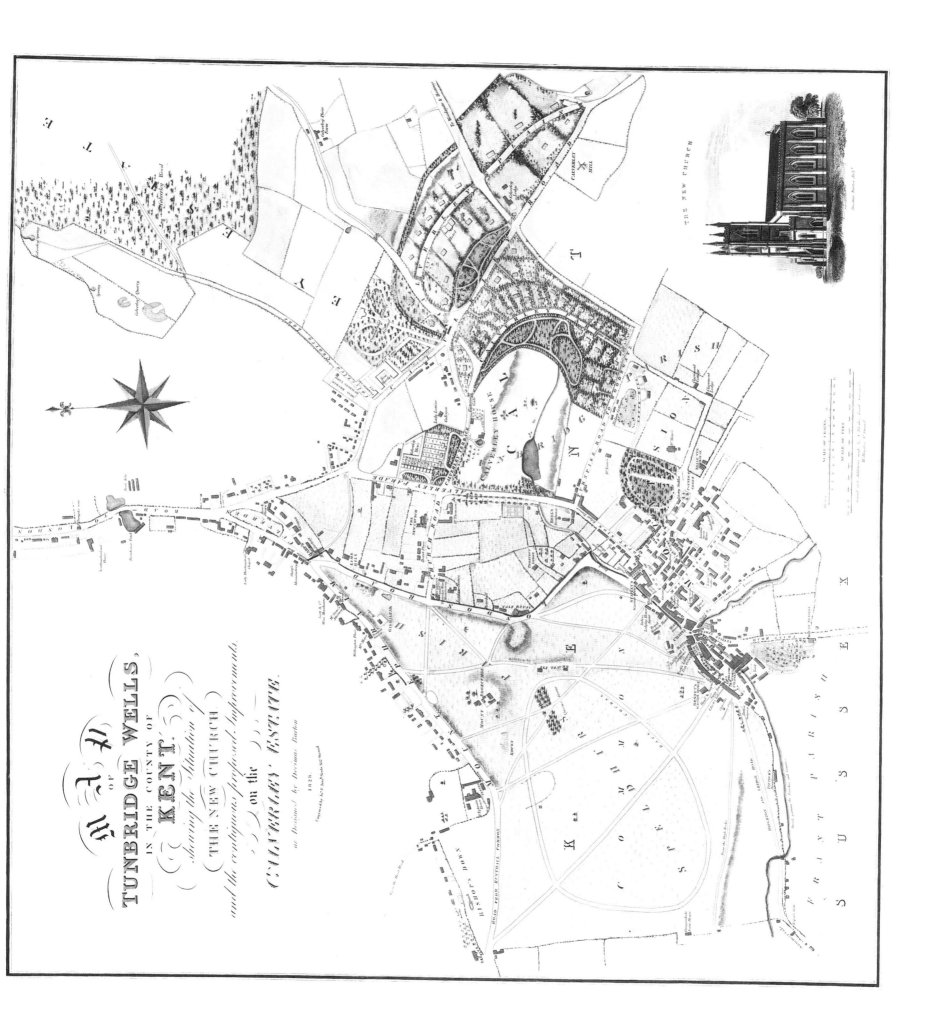

THE NEW CHURCH

MAP
OF
TUNBRIDGE WELLS,
IN THE COUNTY OF
KENT,
shewing the Situation of
THE NEW CHURCH
and the contiguous proposed Improvements.
on the
CALVERLEY ESTATE
as Designed by Decimus Burton
1828.

EDWARD STAVELEY & H.M. WOOD

Nottingham

This plan of the town and county of the town of Nottingham, and of the several extra Parochial Places with the liberties of the castle, together with parts of the Parishes of Lenton, Radford and Sneinton, in the county of Nottingham, From Surveys, made in the Years 1827, 1828 & 1829 . . .

Separate publication, published by Staveley and Wood in Nottingham and Riddle and Co in London, in 1830.
Steel envraving, two sheets, each 585 × 1,155mm.

Nottingham lies 124 miles from London; in 1831 its population was 40,414. Nottingham is an ancient borough and county town, on the north side of the Trent, on the great road from London to Sheffield and Leeds, and at nearly equal distances from Berwick-upon-Tweed on the north and Southampton on the south.

The town is built on a steep rock of soft sandstone, easily excavated, and hence it derives its name, given by the Saxons, who, when they settled here, found a number of caverns, hollowed out of the lower part of the rock, which appeared to have been used as dwellings by the ancient inhabitants; from which it was called 'Snotenagham' or 'Place of Dens'.

The situation of the town is extremely beautiful, the streets being ranged like terraces on the acclivity of a hill which overlooks an extensive tract of country. At the top of this eminence, westwards of the town, stands the castle, the property of the Duke of Newcastle. Several of the streets of this town are wide, airy, and well-paved, considerable modern improvements having taken place here; and within these few years some handsome streets have been built in that part of the town called Standard Hill.

For the manufacture of cotton and silk hosiery the town has long been noted, but those of bobbin-net and various kinds of lace, more recently introduced, also furnish employment for a vast number of persons. Among the other branches of industry prosecuted here are silk throwing and dyeing, hat-making, iron- and brass-founding, nail-making, needle-making, and rope- and twine-making. Tanning, which seems to have been anciently the staple trade of the town, was carried on so extensively in the middle of the seventeenth century, that there were then 47 master tanners; but the number at present is comparatively inconsiderable. Though great quantities of malt are still made here, the brewing of Nottingham ale, for which the town was noted, appears to be now confined to private persons or tavern-keepers.

Markets, Wednesday and Saturday. Fairs on Friday after January 13th, May 7th, the Thursday before Easter, and October 2nd (the Goose Fair). At these fairs, besides other articles, are sold vast quantities of cheese.

NOTTINGHAM

EAST VIEW OF NOTTINGHAM CASTLE.

THOMAS MOULE

The environs of London

Such has been the rapid enlargement of this vast metropolis, which has become connected with places formerly distinct, that it is by no means an easy task to determine its extent or assign its boundaries.

London's dimensions at present may be stated as being about seven miles and a half from the east end of Blackwall to Hyde Park Corner, and nearly four miles from Kings Cross in the north to Kennington Cross in the south. London contains about 9,000 streets, lanes, terraces, &c.; 80 squares, 24 market places, and more than 180,000 houses. The architectural alterations, augmentations and improvements of the metropolis since 1800 are numerous and important beyond those of any former limited period. In 1811 commenced the erection of the magnificent bridge from the Strand across the Thames, which was finished in 1817; an iron bridge leading from Pimlico and Chelsea to Vauxhall was completed and opened in 1816; another iron bridge from the bottom of Thames Street to Bankside, in 1819; and a noble stone bridge, designed to replace the old London Bridge, was completed and opened to the public August 1st, 1831.

The commerce of London is more than commensurate with its importance in other respects. It appears that more merchant ships sail from its port than from all other places in the world, so that it has truly become what it was styled several centuries ago 'the great Emporium of Nations'. It has been computed that the total value of the property shipped and unshipped on the Thames exceeds £70,000,000. With regard to inland commerce it is calculated that more than 40,000 waggons, vans, &c. arrive and depart annually occasioning a traffic of goods worth more than £50,000,000.

The arts and manufactures of London can be at present but briefly noticed. In London are made agricultural machines and implements, surgeons' instruments, artificial hands, legs and eyes, copying machines, needles, for the manufacture of which Whitechapel was formerly noted, fishing tackle, sold chiefly in Crooked Lane, guns and pistols, works in ivory, tortoiseshell, and mother of pearl, artificial flowers and feathers, optical and mathematical instruments, engines for drawing beer, the curious and useful invention of a Mr Dalby, locks on an improved construction invented by Mr Bramah, floor cloths and painted window blinds.

In 1820, there were 30,422 baptisms, 12,757 marriages and 24,367 burials.

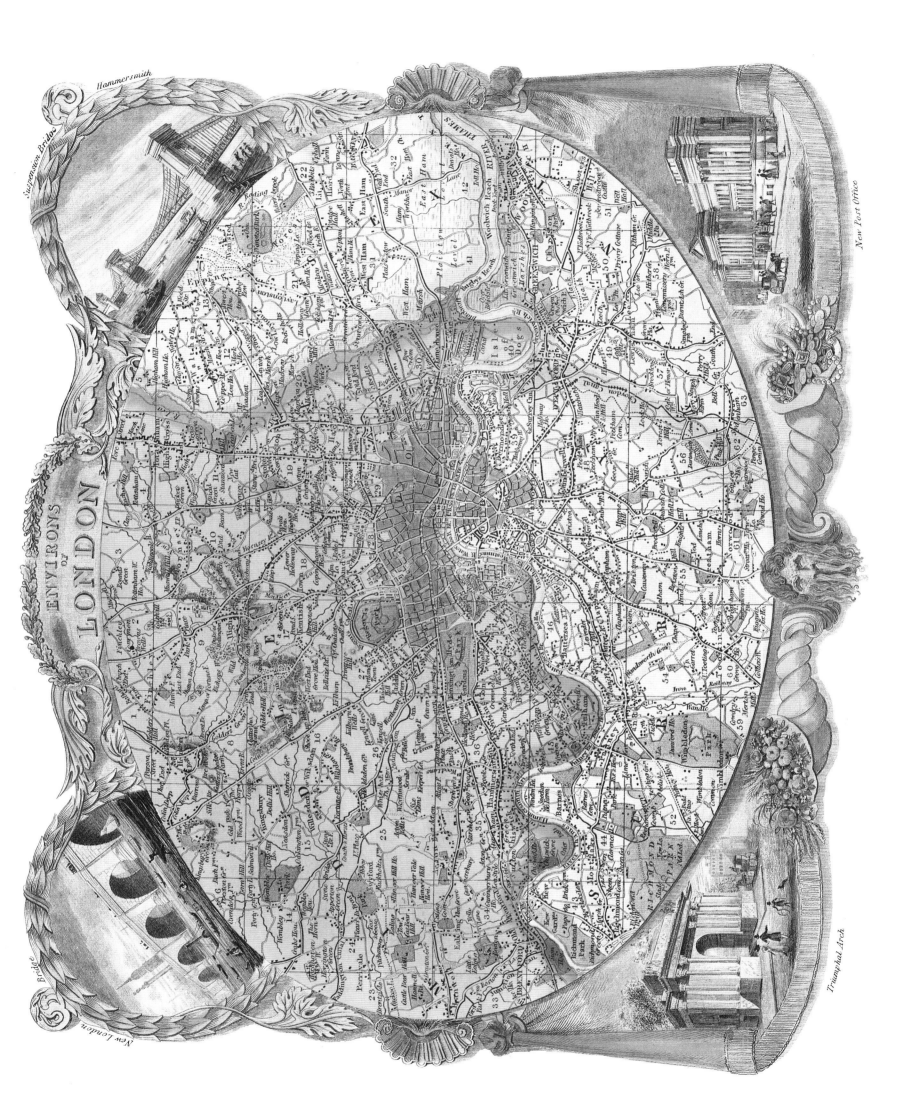

ENVIRONS OF LONDON

THOMAS MOULE

City of Bath

The city of Bath lies 106 miles from London, and has a population of 38,304. This city is aptly built in a pleasant vale, and partly on the acclivity of the hills which arise like an amphitheatre around it. The River Avon winds through a considerable portion of the city and suburbs.

Although, owing to the sanative properties of its waters, Bath has, from the Saxon times downwards, been visited by more sovereigns than any other town in the kingdom, with the exception of the metropolis; it was in other respects a comparatively small and inconsequential place until the commencement of the last century. From that time the city has steadily maintained the lead as relates to the conventional arrangements adapted to places of fashionable resort; and its attraction increasing with its character, the extension of buildings commenced which has gradually rendered it one of the handsomest cities in Europe. On the Landsdowne and Claverton Hills, in particular, handsome ranges of houses are seen rising one above another.

Of the ancient part of the city, the most interesting object is the abbey church, founded by Bishop Oliver King in 1495. It is in the ornamental Gothic style of that late period. The Public Baths, the origin of all the importance of the city, are now in number five, all of which are fitted up and prepared for the accommodation of the highest ranks of society. The spring and fall of the year are the seasons for bathing. As might be expected, the major part of the inhabitants of Bath are dependent on visitors; lodging-houses and accommodations for every rank of which abound. Persons employed in the ornamental lines of business are of course very numerous, and as many families resort to this city for the advantage of the superior education, which its various scholastic establishments afford. Masters of languages, professors of music, and of every species of accompaniment are settled in Bath.

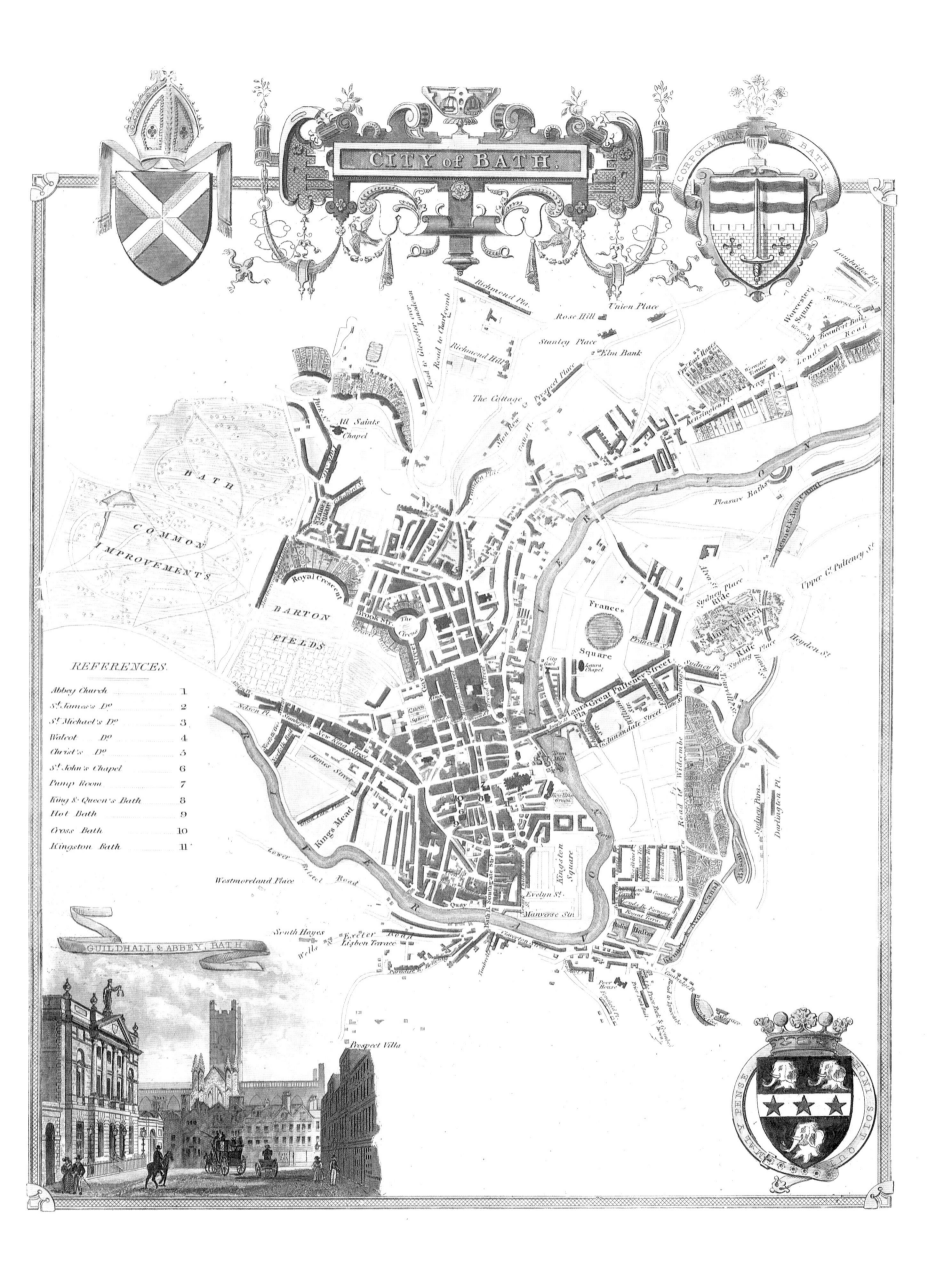

CITY of BATH.

CORPORATION OF BATH

REFERENCES.

Abbey Church	1
St. James's Do	2
St. Michael's Do	3
Walcot Do	4
Christ's Do	5
St. John's Chapel	6
Pump Room	7
King & Queen's Bath	8
Hot Bath	9
Cross Bath	10
Kingston Bath	11

GUILDHALL & ABBEY, BATH.

Boston

Boston lies 116 miles from London, and has a population of 12,942. A sea-port and market town in Lincolnshire, it is situated on each side of the River Witham, near its confluence with the sea. The town has been much improved of late years, by the erection of new houses, by the deepening of the river, and by the enlargement of the harbour, and the erection of a handsome bridge across the river, consisting of one arch, eighty-six feet in the span.

The market-place, which is spacious, is ornamented by a handsome cross, and in the town-hall are commodious assembly rooms. The church is a spacious and interesting pile of architecture, and it is generally believed that its handsome tower was built after the model of that of the great church at Antwerp. At the summit of this tower is a beautiful lanthorn, which serves as a sea-mark in the dangerous navigation of the Boston and Lynn deeps. It is supposed to be the largest church without cross aisles in the kingdom.

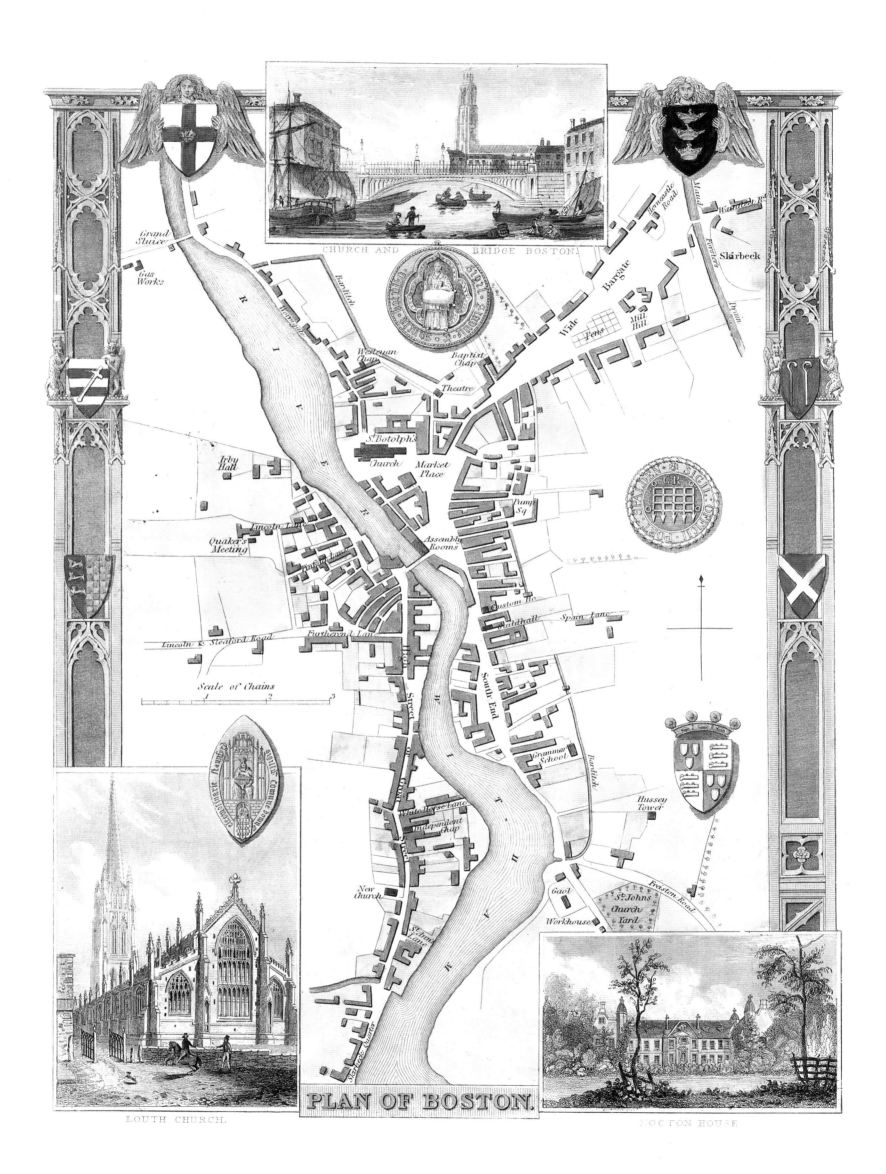

CHURCH AND BRIDGE BOSTON.

Grand Sluice
Gas Works
Baptists
Hornadle
Wesleyan Chap.
Baptist Chap.
Theatre
St Botolphs Church
Market Place
Irby Hall
Lincoln Lane
Quaker's Meeting
Pinfold Lane
Lincoln & Sleaford Road
Furthernd Lan.
Scale of Chains
Assembly Rooms
Pump Sq
Custom Ho
Guildhall
Spain Lane
High Street
South End
Bargate
Wide
Fens
Mill Hill
Horncastle Road
Maud
Warwick Rd
Fosters
Skirbeck
Drain
Grammar School
Bargate
Hussey Tower
White Horse Lane
Independent Chap
New Church
St Ann's Lane
Gaol
Workhouse
St Johns Church Yard
Preston Road
Market Quarter

PLAN OF BOSTON.

LOUTH CHURCH.

NOCTON HOUSE.

THOMAS MOULE

Cambridge

Cambridge is 51 miles from London; its population is 24,453. It is the county town and seat of a celebrated university, and is situated on the river Cam, which divides it into two unequal parts. The university contains 13 colleges and 4 halls. Its buildings are elegant, and its libraries and cabinets valuable and extensive. The Fitzwilliam Museum, Senate House, Observatory, &c., are connected with it. The town-hall and county-hall are the only buildings of note that do not appertain to the university. The streets are narrow, but well paved, and the houses are old; the market-place is spacious, and in it is a handsome stone conduit, to which water is conveyed by an aqueduct. It communicates with London and the north by railway.

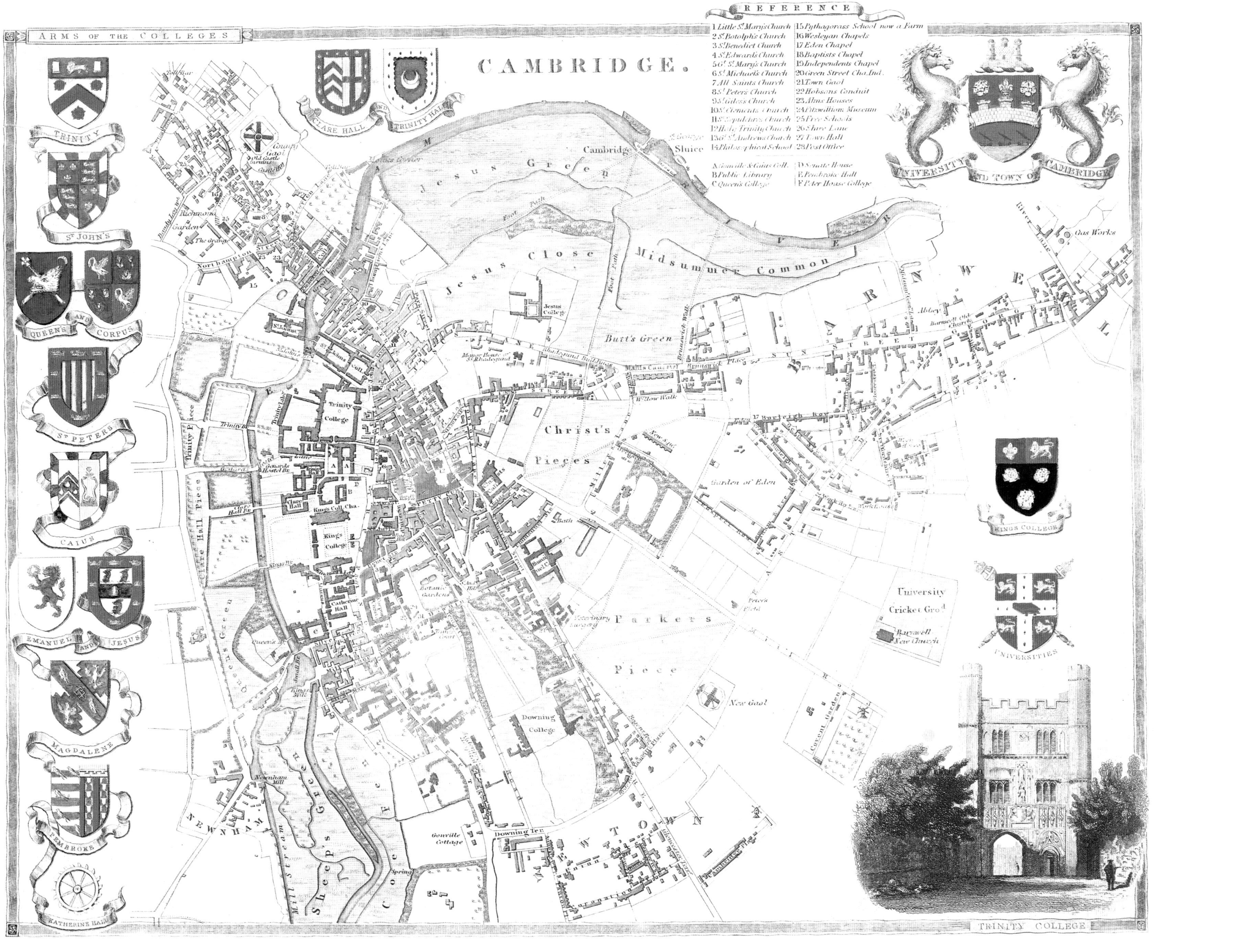

CAMBRIDGE.
ARMS OF THE COLLEGES
REFERENCE
1 Little S.t Mary's Church
2 S.t Botolph's Church
3 S.t Benedict Church
4 S.t Edward's Church
5 G.t S.t Mary's Church
6 S.t Michael's Church
7 All Saints Church
8 S.t Peter's Church
9 S.t Giles's Church
10 S.t Clements Church
11 S.t Sepulchre's Church
12 Holy Trinity Church
13 G.t S.t Andrews Church
14 Philosophical School
15 Pythagorass School now a Farm
16 Wesleyan Chapels
17 Eden Chapel
18 Baptists Chapel
19 Independents Chapel
20 Green Street Cha. Ind.
21 Town Gaol
22 Hobsons Conduit
23 Alms Houses
24 Fitzwilliam Museum
25 Free Schools
26 Shire Lane
27 Town Hall
28 Post Office
A Gonville & Caius Coll.
B Public Library
C Queen's College
D Senate House
E Pembroke Hall
F Peter House College
UNIVERSITY AND TOWN OF CAMBRIDGE
TRINITY
S.T JOHN'S
QUEEN'S AND CORPUS
S.T PETERS
CAIUS
EMANUEL AND JESUS
MAGDALENE
PEMBROKE
KATHERINE HALL
CLARE HALL AND TRINITY HALL
KINGS COLLEGE
UNIVERSITIES
TRINITY COLLEGE
Jesus Green
Jesus Close
Midsummer Common
Butt's Green
Christ's Pieces
Parkers Piece
Garden of Eden
University Cricket Grod
Barnwell New Church
New Gaol
Covent Garden
Trinity College
Kings College
Jesus College
Downing College
Gonville Cottage
Downing Ter.
Clare Hall Piece
Trinity Piece
Queens Green
Sheeps Green
Mill Stream
Newnham Mill
NEWNHAM
Gas Works
River Lane
Cambridge Sluice
Northampton Street
Richmond Garden
The Grange
Botanic Gardens
Catherine Hall
Clare Hall
Queen's Coll.
BARNWELL
NEW TOWN

THOMAS MOULE

The City and University of Oxford

Oxford is 51 miles from London; its population is 23,834. It is seated at the confluence of the Thames and Cherwell, on an eminence almost surrounded by meadows, except on the eastern side. The whole town, with the suburbs, is of a circular form, 3 miles in circumference. It consists chiefly of two spacious streets, which cross each other in the middle of the town.

It is celebrated for its university, which is said to have been founded by Alfred, but is generally supposed to have been of even earlier origin. Here are 20 colleges, and 5 halls, several of which stand in the streets, and give the city an air of magnificence, which has obtained for it the name of the 'City of Cathedrals'. The colleges are very wealthy, but are retained exclusively by the Established Church. The number of students is usually about 2,000. Among the libraries in the university, the most distinguished is the Bodleian, founded by Thomas Bodley; those of All Souls' College, Christ Church, Queen's, New College, St John's, Exeter, and Corpus Christi. Among other public buildings, are the Theatre, the Ashmolean Museum, the Clarendon Printing-house, the Radcliffe Infirmary, and a fine Observatory.

Markets, Wednesday and Saturday.

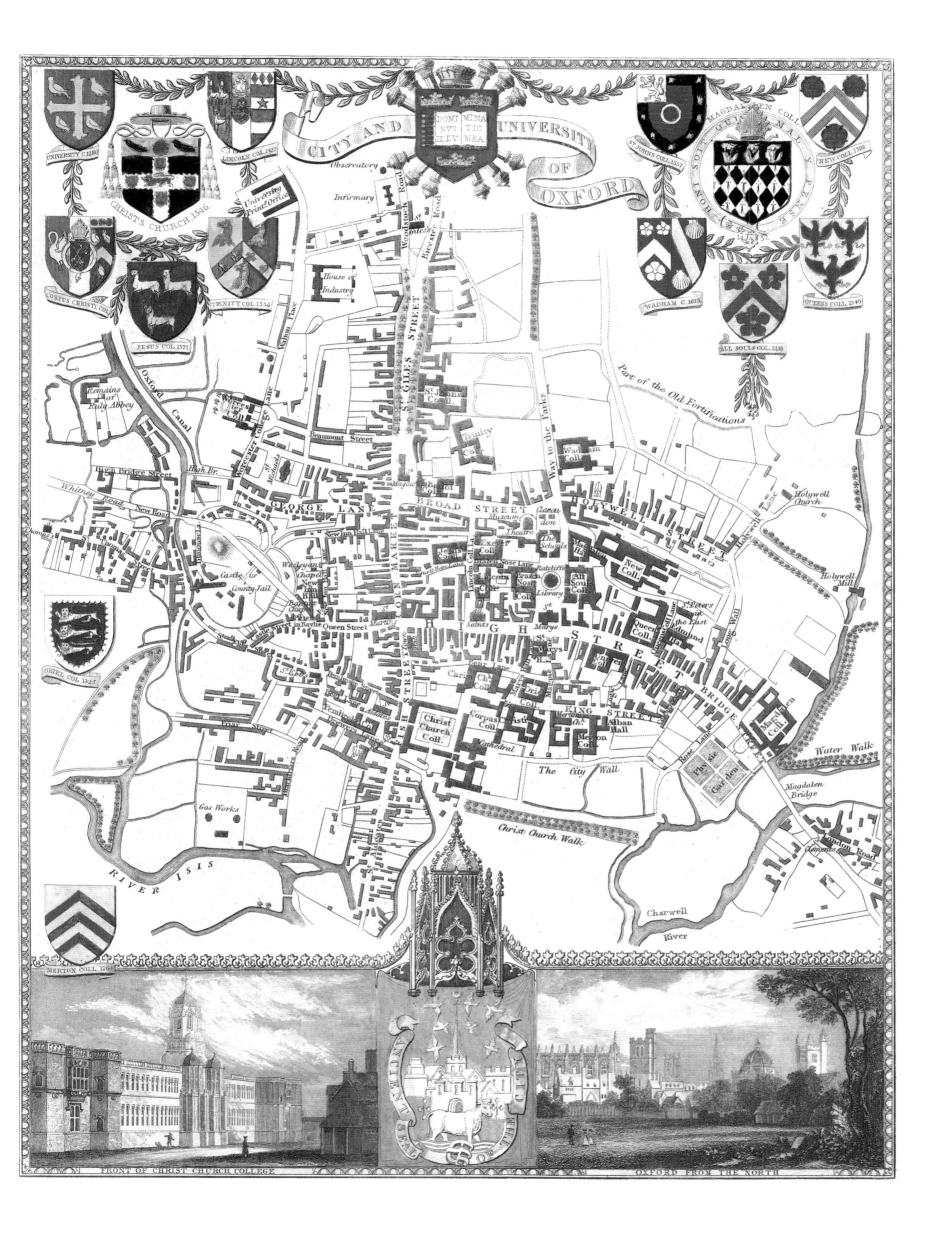

CITY AND UNIVERSITY OF OXFORD

DOMI NVS NVS TIO ILLV MEA

UNIVERSITY C.1280

LINCOLN COL. 1427

CHRIST'S CHURCH. 1546

University Printg Office

CORPUS CHRISTI COL.

TRINITY COL. 1554

JESUS COL. 1571

ST JOHNS COLL. 1557

MAGDALEN COLL.

HON SOIT QVI MAL Y PENSE

WADHAM C. 1613.

ALL SOULS COL. 1438

NEW COLL. 1386

QUEEN'S COLL. 1340

ORIEL COL. 1325

MERTON COLL. 1264

Observatory

Infirmary

Remains of Rewly Abbey

Oxford Canal

House of Industry

Beaumont Street

Worcester College Lane

Walton Place

High Bridge Street   High Br.

Whitney Road

New Road

St Michaels

GEORGE LANE

Magdalen

St Giles Street

Leicester Road

Woodstock Road

St Johns Coll.

Trinity Coll.

Way to the Parks

Wadham Coll.

Part of the Old Fortifications

BROAD STREET

Museum

Theatre

Clarendon

The Schools

HOLYWELL STREET

Holywell Church

Holywell Lane

Holywell Mill

Castle or County Jail

Wesleyan Chapel

New Inn Hall

Baptist Chapel

Exeter Coll.

Jesus Coll.

Lincoln Coll.

Brazen Nose Coll.

Radcliffe Library

All Souls Coll.

New Coll.

Long Wall

S. Peters in the East

Queen's Coll.

St Edmund Hall

HIGH STREET

Queen Street

Tower

Carfax

St Martys

All Saints

St Marys

University Coll.

Bear Lane

Merton Lane

Magdalen Coll.

Castle Street in Bayly   Queen Street

St Ebbs

St Ebbs

Pembroke Coll.

St Aldates

Christ Church Coll.

Corpus Christi Coll.

Oriel Coll.

Merton Ch.

Alban Hall

Magdalen Coll.

KING STREET

Cathedral

Rose Lane

Physic Garden

Water Walk

Magdalen Bridge

Gas Works

RIVER ISIS

The City Wall

Christ Church Walk

Charwell River

London Road

ANCIENT SEAL OF THE

FRONT OF CHRIST CHURCH COLLEGE

OXFORD FROM THE NORTH

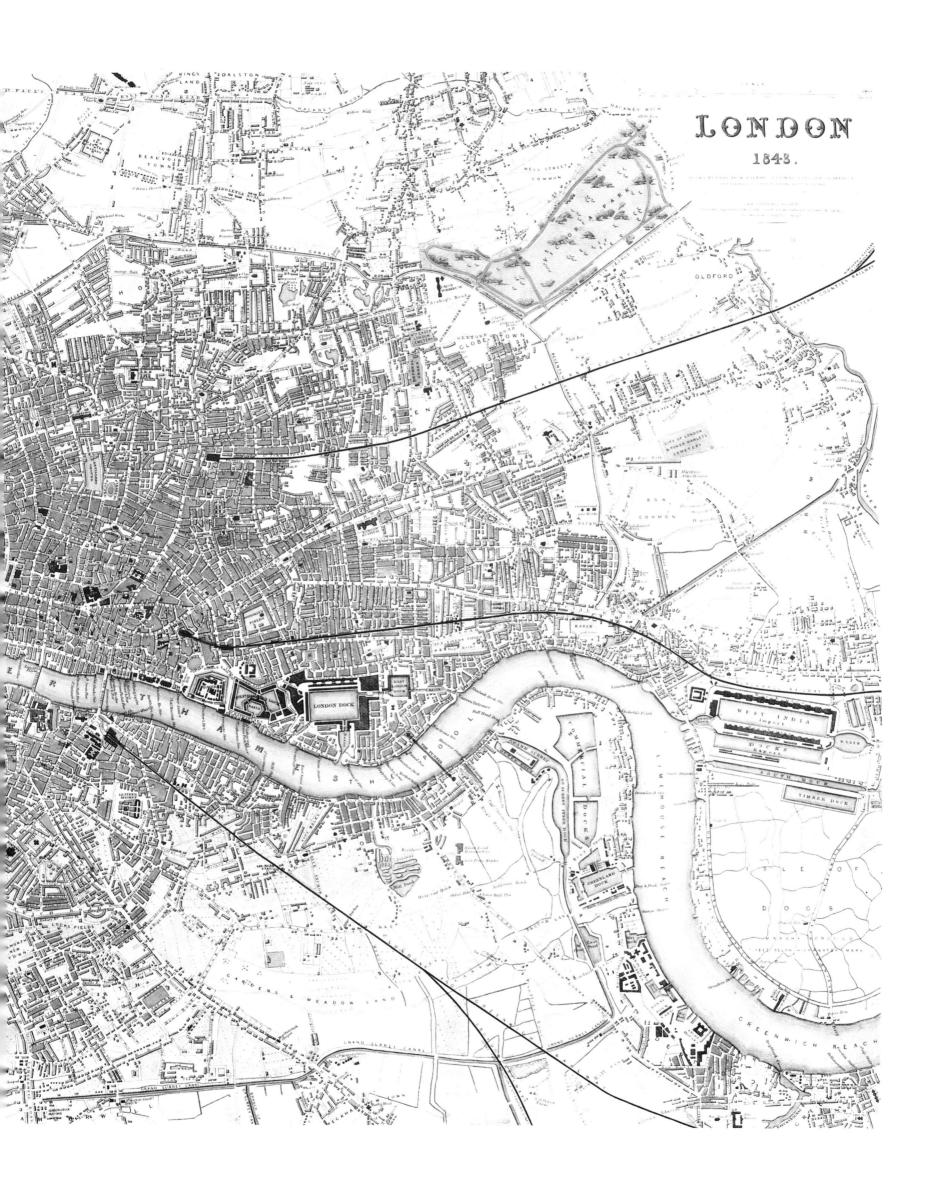

LONDON
1843.

London

The population of London in 1833 was 1,274,800. The metropolis of the United Kingdom of Great Britain and Ireland, and of the British Empire, stands on the Thames, which is crossed by eight bridges, and under which a tunnel has been driven; extends from Woolwich and Bow to Fulham and Hammersmith, and from Highgate to Norwood, including the cities of London and Westminster, with their liberties, and the towns parishes, &c., &c. which cover this vast area. The streets of the city, with the exception of the great thoroughfares, are for the most part narrow and irregular; but the main lines of traffic and communication are wide and noble, as are the more recently built parts of this enormous city.

The public edifices are innumerable, and for magnificence may vie with those of any city in the world. St Paul's Cathedral stands pre-eminent amongst these, built by Sir Christopher Wren which, though it is most disadvantageously situated, being closely surrounded by houses, and is said not to have been the edifice Sir Christopher had hoped to raise, is yet sufficiently imposing in appearance. Many of the other churches are very noble buildings, but most of them are in by-streets.

Of the government and public buildings, the New Palace of Westminster, the remains of Whitehall, the Horse-Guards, Admiralty, and other connected public offices, the Post-Office, the Royal Exchange, the Mansion House, the Custom House, Somerset House, the India House, Lincoln's Inn Buildings, and those of the Temple and other Inns of Court, the British Museum, the Bank (for the notion of complete security against unauthorized ingress), the prison of Newgate (for the notion of equal security against unauthorized egress), the National Gallery (for the exhibition of no notion at all), the Theatres, the Colosseum, the Hospitals, the Bazaars, the Railway Termini, deserve special notice and mention.

Yet perhaps these are not, though they first meet the eye, the most astonishing features of the British metropolis. The prodigious docks, with their immense bonding-warehouses, the warehouses of the city, towering into the air, and sinking deeply into the earth, convey the notion of wealth and commerce completely stupendous. Vast manufactories of almost all kinds of commodities, which are hardly recognized in the endless crowds of buildings, make London, in this respect, the rival of whole provinces. By means of the river, London ranks as the first port of the kingdom; canals enable it to communicate, for the transit of heavy goods, with all the interior of the country; whilst railways, branching out in every direction, bring the remotest counties into closest proximity with this emporium of the world, for goods of more perishable character or lighter carriage, and for travellers. Here are six parks (including Greenwich Park), which are open to the public. The squares, which are usually ornamentally planted, are of great advantage to some districts, in regard to health. But the parts of the metropolis inhabited by the poorer classes are yet the prolific sources of disease; and the retention of Smithfield market and the slaughter-houses in the very heart of London must also be noticed as a heavy drawback on the health, safety, and even morality of the city.

For every species of rational and intelligent recreation, London stands pre-eminent; theatres, concert-rooms, museums, lecture-rooms, and scientific institutions. It is also the centre of the literary world. Of the numberless charitable and religious institutions it is impossible to make any mention. The City of London is under the control of a corporation, of enormous wealth; whose practical inefficiency, and steadfast resistance of all reformation or change, are matters of painful notoriety. Several regiments of cavalry and infantry are customarily quartered in or near the metropolis but chiefly for state purposes, and occasions of royal pomp; the guardianship of the streets and the public peace and safety are committed to a numerous and well-appointed body of police. The whole of the district is also well lighted with gas, and well supplied with spring water, by various companies.

Birmingham

Birmingham is 116 miles from London. The population in 1833 was 85,416, and with Aston and Edgbaston, 106,722. Mail arrived 7.58pm, and departed 5.07am. A market-town, situated on the side of a hill, by the River Rea, in the north-western extremity of the county of Warwickshire. Birmingham was a place of some consideration at the time of the Conquest; and gave name to the ancient family of Birmingham, but the town is not associated with any historical events of much importance.

The chief street of the ancient town is that called Digbeth, which is in a low and watery situation. The more modern portion is, on the contrary, approached by an ascent on every side, except the north-west. So prodigious has been the diffusion of building, that from 1700 to 1821 the number of houses increased from 2,504 to 17,323. The town is now two miles long, and new houses are continually building. A new street leading from Worcester Street to Bromsgrove Street, has been recently laid out; new lines of communication have been opened between Lower Ashted and various parts of the town and its environs; and from Bell-barn Road to the Five Ways; and from the Bristol road to Balsall Heath. Here are two crosses, the one called the Welsh, and the other the High Cross, over which the Court of Requests is held. Great improvements are now proceeding, especially in the construction of a new and enlarged market, for which many houses have been taken down under the authority of an act of Parliament, in High Street, Spiceal Street, Bell Street, Philip Street, and Worcester Street. It is expected that when all shall have been completed, no town in England will excel Birmingham in these conveniences.

The town is watched, paved, and lighted with gas, under the provision of a recent Act of Parliament. The flagging of the footpaths is gradually proceeding, and the edging of the flags with scored iron curbs, the invention of a native of the town, adds both to its neatness and durability.

As regards the manufacturing importance of this town, it was celebrated for the skill of its smiths and artisans in ironware so early as the reign of Henry VIII. It was not until the reign of Charles II, however, when the toy trade began to flourish, that the career of ingenuity and industry was entered upon which has acquired for Birmingham such a high degree of manufacturing renown. It was in the reign of William III that muskets were first made here, which business during the late war [the Napoleonic War] was carried on to an immense extent. Working in brass was introduced in 1740, and one branch after another from time to time, until every species of hardware, plated articles, jewellery, trinket and toy-making was, as at present, included.

The inland position of this large town might have been unfavourable to the transaction of business on a large scale, but owing to the extension of canal navigation this difficulty has long been superseded. The old canal opens a communication with the Severn to Shrewsbury, Gloucester and Bristol, and by the Trent to Gainsborough, Hull and London. A junction has also been made between this canal and the grand line running through the Staffordshire potteries to Manchester and Liverpool; thus opening a water communication to the leading ports in both seas. The new Birmingham or Fazeley Canal provides a similar water conveyance by Tamworth, Atherston, Nuneaton and Coventry, to Oxford; and thence by the Thames to London. The central position of this town is also highly favourable to its commercial and manufacturing prosperity.

Although forges and furnaces so much abound, the air of Birmingham is deemed pure and salubrious, which is possibly owing to the dryness of its red and sandy soil. The vicinity abounds with many pleasant villas and retreats of its opulent manufacturers.

BIRMINGHAM

Published under the Superintendence of the Society for the
Diffusion of Useful Knowledge.

SCALE.
2 Furlongs or ¼ of a Mile
Yards

PLAN OF BIRMINGHAM AND ITS ENVIRONS
with the Boundaries taken from the Reform Act

EXPLANATIONS.
Boundary of Borough
Boundaries of Parishes or Townsh~
Boundaries of Wards

Scale of Miles

REFERENCE TO THE WARDS
All Saints   1
Hockley   2
St Georges   3
St Martins   4
Duddeston and Nechels   5
Deritend and Bordesley 6
St Martins   7
St Thomas's   8
Lady Wood   9
Market Hall   10
St Peters   11
St Pauls   12
Edgbaston   13

Dublin

The population of Dublin in 1831 was 185,881; it is 331½ miles from London, via Holyhead. The metropolis of Ireland, Dublin is situated upon the Anna Liffey, i.e. the swift river. The ancient Irish called it Dubhlin, from Dubh, black, and llyn, a pool, being situated upon a dark-looking marsh or pool.

The public buildings, the leading avenues, the many beautiful squares, and the numerous and splendid private mansions of Dublin are alone sufficient to establish its reputation as one of the most elegant cities in Europe. It is sometimes compared with Berlin, and Edinburgh has lately been brought forward as its rival. But it will not be necessary to depress either place, in order to establish the just claim which this city is acknowledged to possess. The noblest city avenue in Europe is Sackville Street; it is broader and longer than Portland Place, in London, and the houses, formerly the mansions of the resident nobility, are loftier and more architectural. Stephen's Green, the largest square in any known city, exceeds one mile in circumference.

The public buildings are of the first class, whether the classical design or the magnitude and workmanship be taken as the criterion. The streets are well paved and lighted with gas, of which there are extensive works, one for oil, the other of coal gas, with the latter of which the city is lighted.

The trade of Dublin is various and extensive. As a place of exportation it is increasing daily, and will be the chief corn market in the kingdom; cattle and hides are also exported in great quantities; and lately Dublin porter has grown into much estimation, and is imported into the west and south of England. The bar, at the entrance to the harbour, militates against the admission of vessels of large burden, and consequently diminishes trade; a few West Indiamen, however, trade regularly with this port. The great and valuable business is transacted with Liverpool, Bristol, and London by steamers, as well as by windborne vessels. The river is only navigable as far as the Carlisle Bridge, but here are noble wet-docks, capable of floating some hundred sail, besides two canals, extending from the River Liffey to the River Shannon, by means of which waterways the agricultural produce of the midland counties is carried to Dublin at a cheap and expeditious rate, and there shipped for the English market.

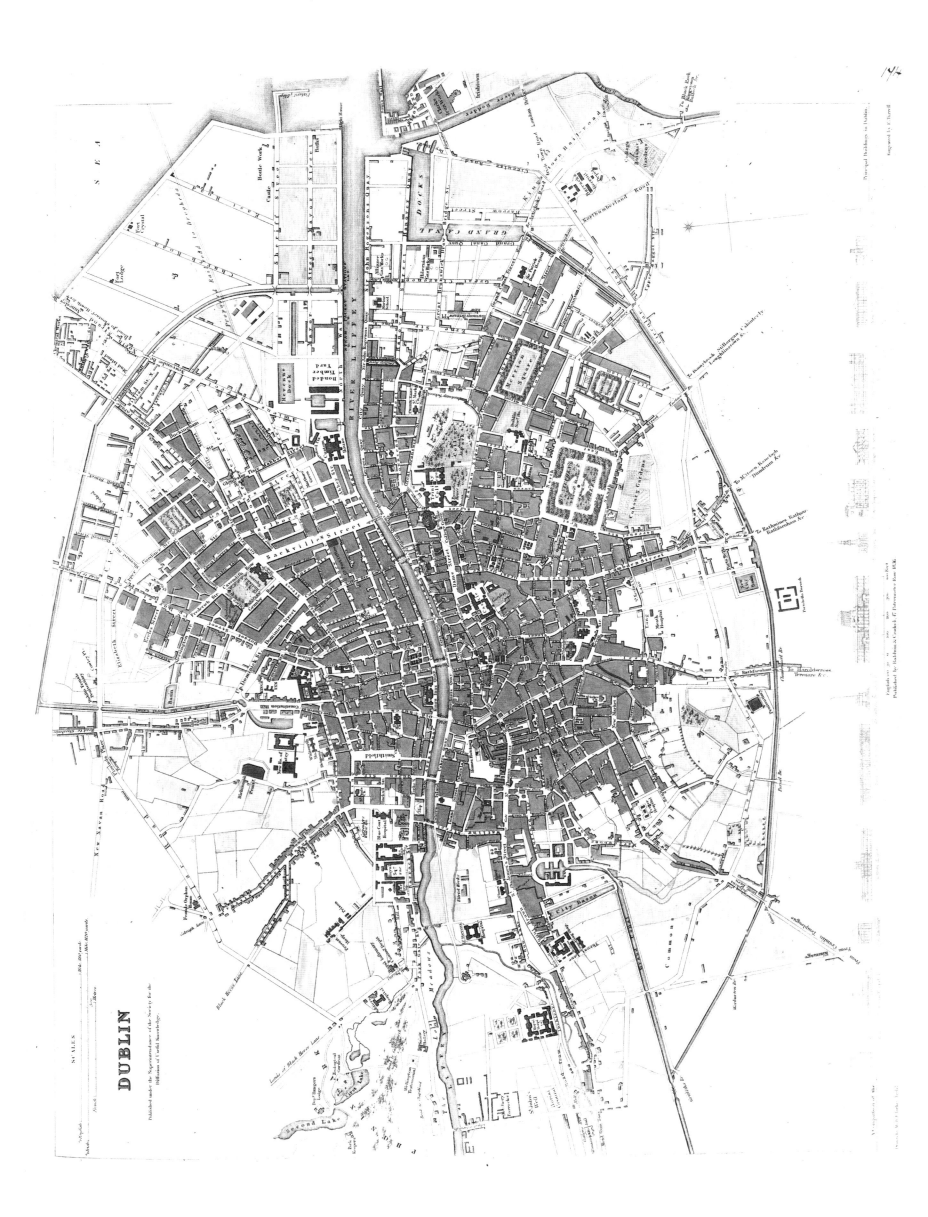

DUBLIN

Published under the Superintendence of the Society for the
Diffusion of Useful Knowledge.

Edinburgh

Edinburgh is 377 miles from London, with a population of 138,235. The mail arrives at 3.38am, and departs at 8.00pm. An ancient city, the metropolis of Scotland, and previous to the union of the two kingdoms the seat of government, as it is still of the principal civil and criminal courts of judicature. It stands a mile and a half south of the Firth of Forth; and on every side except the north it is encompassed with lofty hills. To the east are Calton Hill, Arthur's Seat, and Salisbury Craigs; to the south the hills of Braid, and at some distance to the west Corstorphine Hill. These heights afford fine prospects of the city and its environs; and from Arthur's Seat especially, the eye of the spectator commands a panoramic view of vast extent and beauty.

Edinburgh comprises at present two distinct districts, called the Old Town and the New Town, differing greatly in their architecture and arrangement, and consequently in their general character and appearance. In the middle of the last century, what is now called the Old Town constituted the whole city of Edinburgh, which is chiefly built upon a hill of singular form, rising gradually from east to west, and terminated at the latter extremity by a precipitous rock, three hundred feet in height, on which stands the ancient castle. From this fortress the High Street extends eastward along the summit of the ridge to the palace of Holyrood House.

The New Town, which is the peculiar boast and pride of Edinburgh, forms a complete contrast with the Old Town, and as respects regularity of design and beauty of situation, may, perhaps, be considered as the most splendid assemblage of buildings in the kingdom. It consists, however, of two parts, that of which the plan was arranged in 1767, when the ground to the north of the ancient city was added to the royalty of Edinburgh; and the more recent ranges of buildings northward of the preceding, from which they differ less in architectural merit, than in uniformity of arrangement. This part of the city is situated on an elevation, which is divided from the Old Town by a deep valley, formerly a morass called the North Loch; and the communication between the two towns is preserved by the North Bridge, and by an earthen mound or embankment.

The entrance to Edinburgh, from the London road, was formerly through narrow and inconvenient streets; but in 1814 a new road was commenced across the Calton Hill, in one part of which a passage has been cut through the solid rock to facilitate the ascent. Between the Calton Hill and Princes Street a deep ravine intervenes, over which an elegant arch, called Regents Bridge, has been thrown, connecting the hill with Princes Street; and now the road form a fine terrace, affording varied and delightful views of the ancient metropolis of Scotland.

The Castle of Edinburgh is built on a rugged rock, which rises almost perpendicularly on three sides, the entrance to it being from the east quarter, where it is defended by palisades and a dry ditch, over which there is a drawbridge and a gate, flanked by two batteries. Before the invention of gunpowder, this fortress was deemed impregnable, a character to which it has no claim at present. It was a royal residence previously to the union of England and Scotland, and the room is still shown in which James VI was born. The prospect from the castle on every side is grand and beautiful, and to the north very extensive, stretching beyond the Firth of Forth, with its islands and shipping, and taking not only the hills and fields of Fifeshire, but also in clear weather, Ben Lomond.

The manufactures carried on at Edinburgh at present are chiefly such as contribute to support the wants and luxury of the inhabitants; among which may be included the making of cabinet work and various kinds of household furniture, of carriages, and of musical instruments; the linen manufacture of shawls, silks, and sarsenets; those of glass, marble, brass and ironwork. There are also two distilleries on a great scale; and Edinburgh has long been famous for its ale, which is sent to London.

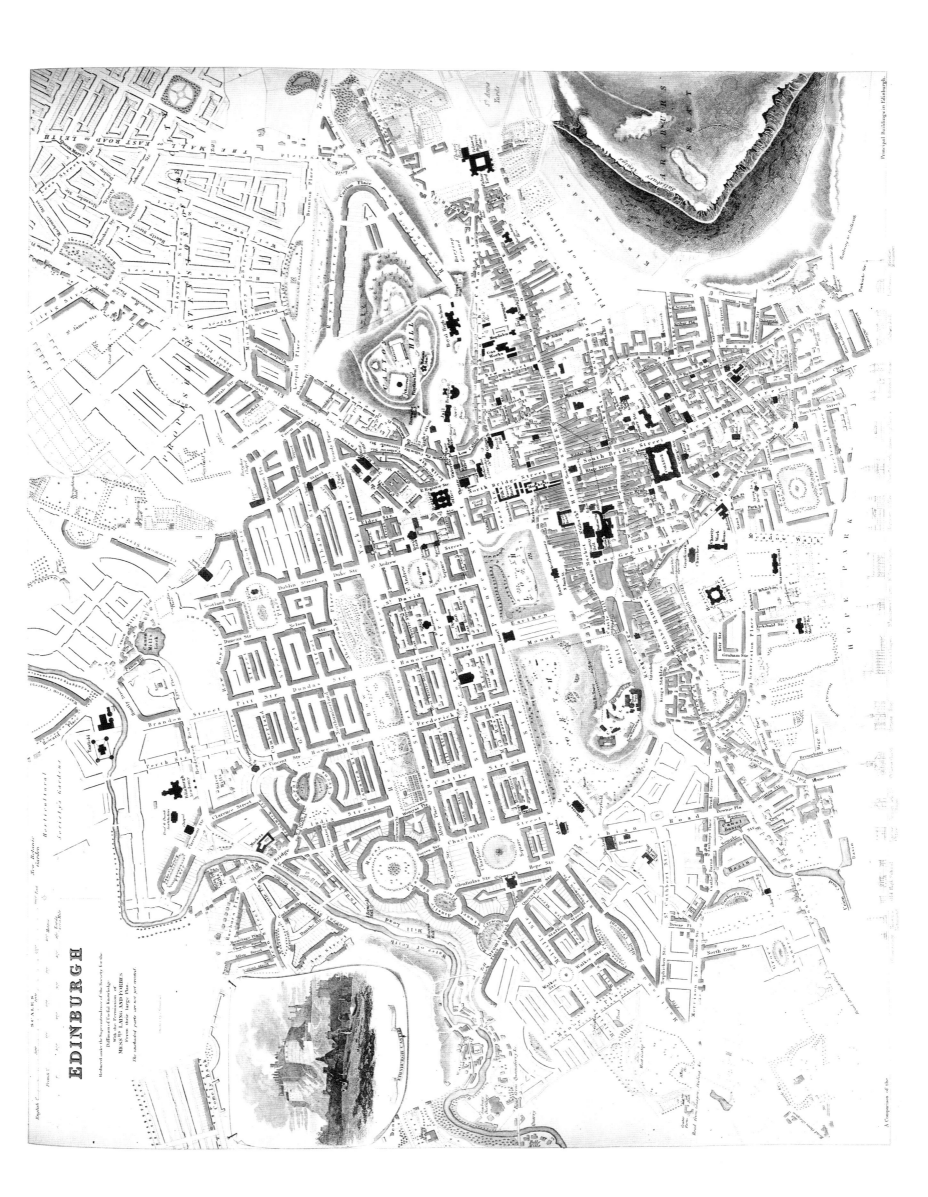

EDINBURGH

Reduced under the Superintendence of the Society for the
Diffusion of Useful Knowledge.
With the Permission of
MESSᴿˢ. LANG AND FORBES
From their large Plan.
The unshaded parts are not yet erected.

Liverpool

Liverpool is 206 miles from London; the population in 1833 was 118,972. This town has risen to its present height of prosperity and importance entirely through the influence of commerce; and in wealth, population, and foreign trade it is inferior to no place in the kingdom, except London. Its ancient history affords but few particulars worthy of note.

The town extends along the eastern bank of the Mersey about three miles, and at an average about a mile inland; but its limits are gradually altering, from the increase of buildings. The most remarkable feature in the town consists of the docks, wharfs, and warehouses, stretching in an immense range along the border of the river. In the opposite direction the town is prolonged into numerous suburbs, consisting chiefly of villas and country-houses, the fixed or occasional residences of the wealthy citizens. The houses in general are built of brick, and roofed with tiles obtained from North Wales. The streets are not arranged in any regular plan, and therefore scarcely admit of description; but among the handsomest and most extensive may be mentioned Castle Street, Dale Street, Paradise Street, Hanover Street, Duke Street, St Anne's Street, and Rodney Street; and there are several squares, which require no particular notice.

Within a few years past several new streets have been completed, spacious, airy, and commodious in their arrangement, with buildings by no means devoid of elegance and regularity of style and construction; and the older and more confined parts of the town, by their progressive improvement, indicate the growing prosperity of this great mart of foreign and domestic commerce.

From October 18th, 1822, to October 18th, 1823, the corporation of Liverpool expended more than £30,000 in improvements of the town and certain repairs, besides £4,525 3s. 6d. towards building St Luke's Church. The streets in general are well paved, and the town is brilliantly lit with gas, under the direction of two joint-stock companies.

Among the public works connected with commerce, one of the most considerable is the Liverpool and Manchester Railway. This railway is carried under the town by two tunnels, extending from the Edgehill to near the Queen's Dock, about 2,200 yards. On the 15th of September, 1830, the works on the whole line having been entirely executed, the railway was opened; on which occasion the Duke of Wellington and many other persons of rank and eminence accompanied the directors of the undertaking in steam carriages prepared for the passage.

In 1800 the whole number of ships which entered this port was 4,746, and the dock duties £23,379 13s. 6d.; in 1823, the number amounted to 8,916, the united burden of which was 1,010,819 tons, the duties paid being £115,783 1s. 6d. In 1829, there were belonging to the port of Liverpool 805 ships, altogether of 161,780 tons burden; being a greater number of vessels and higher amount of tonnage than were possessed by any other port of the united empire, except those of London and Newcastle.

The gross receipt of customs at Liverpool in 1823 was £1,808,402, of which sum the tobacco duty alone amounted to £1,012,857; and the King's Warehouse then contained 12,000 hogsheads of that article; while in the same year were imported 578,300 bags of cotton; and the value of goods deposited in the bonding warehouses has been estimated to be seldom less than £1,500,000 sterling.

In October, 1827, a line of telegraph was completed from Liverpool to Holyhead, by means of which communications may be made from one extremity to the other, a distance of 128 miles in five minutes, and a plan has been proposed for a similar communication with Manchester.

In 1829, the horse-races for the first time were held at Aintree, about 5 miles from Liverpool, and continued during four days. A grand stand has since been erected, enclosed by iron railings, which will contain about 1,500 persons, and the whole building will accommodate about 3,000.

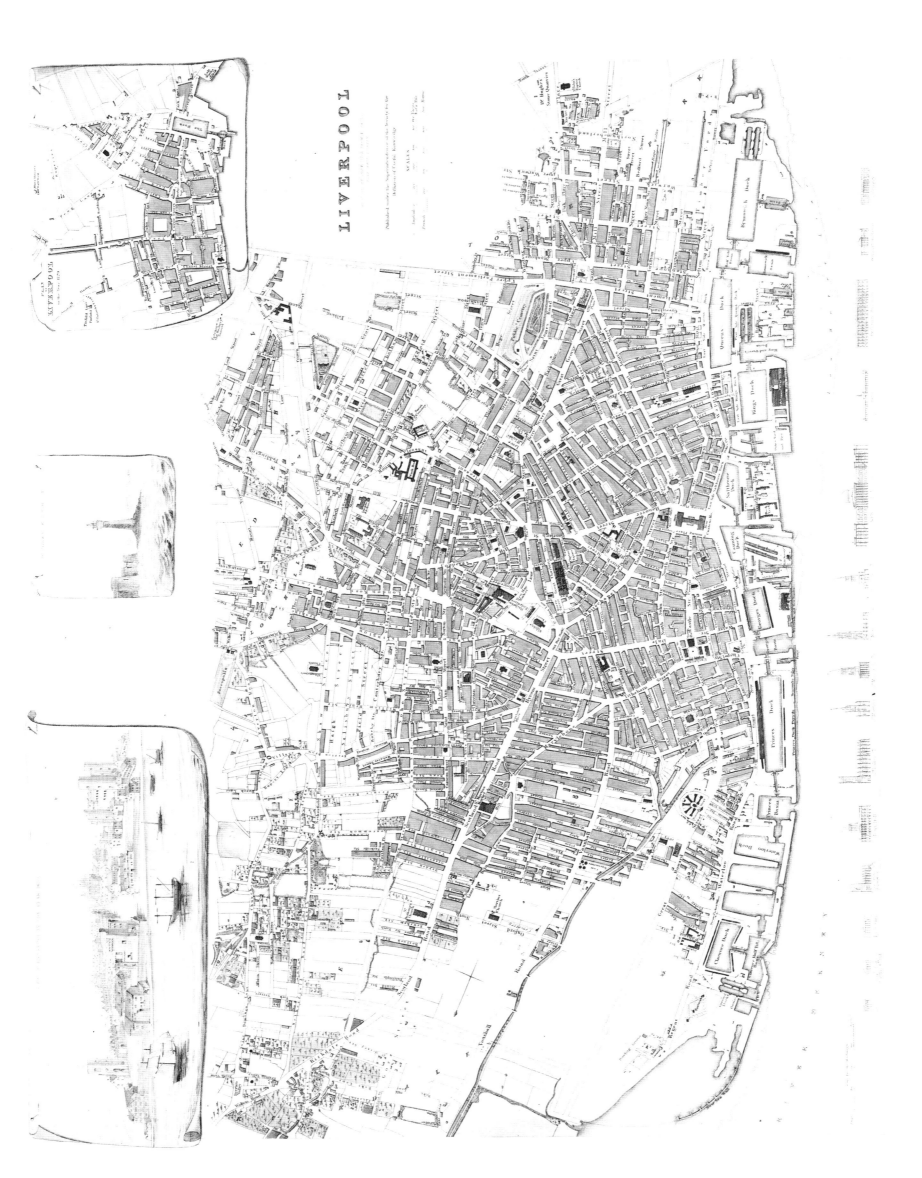

LIVERPOOL

Falmouth

Lithograph, 300 × 260mm.

Falmouth is 269 miles from London; its population is 6,374. A market and sea-port town, seated at the bottom of an eminence commanding the harbour at the mouth of the River Fal, near the English Channel; the houses are principally arranged in one street, which extends along the beach for nearly a mile. The quay here is very convenient, as the water is of sufficient depth to admit vessels of large burden. The harbour is very capacious, and affords excellent security for ships, being well screened by the surrounding high lands.

Falmouth owes its origin to an individual who built a small cottage where she sold beer to the sailors coming onshore. From the quickness of the sale of this beverage, it was long called Penny Come Quick. This however, having been thought a good situation for trading, John Killigrew, in 1613, formed a grand plan of building a whole town here, and very soon formed a considerable town of good buildings. Thus, in little more than two centuries, from being a very small village, consisting of only a few fishing huts, Falmouth has become one of the most considerable towns in this county.

It owes the great increase in its commercial importance in the last century to the packet boats stationed here for Spain, Portugal, and almost all parts of the World. It carries on a considerable fishery in pilchards, which is also a source of great emolument to some of the inhabitants.

FALMOUTH

Enlarged from the Ordnance Survey.

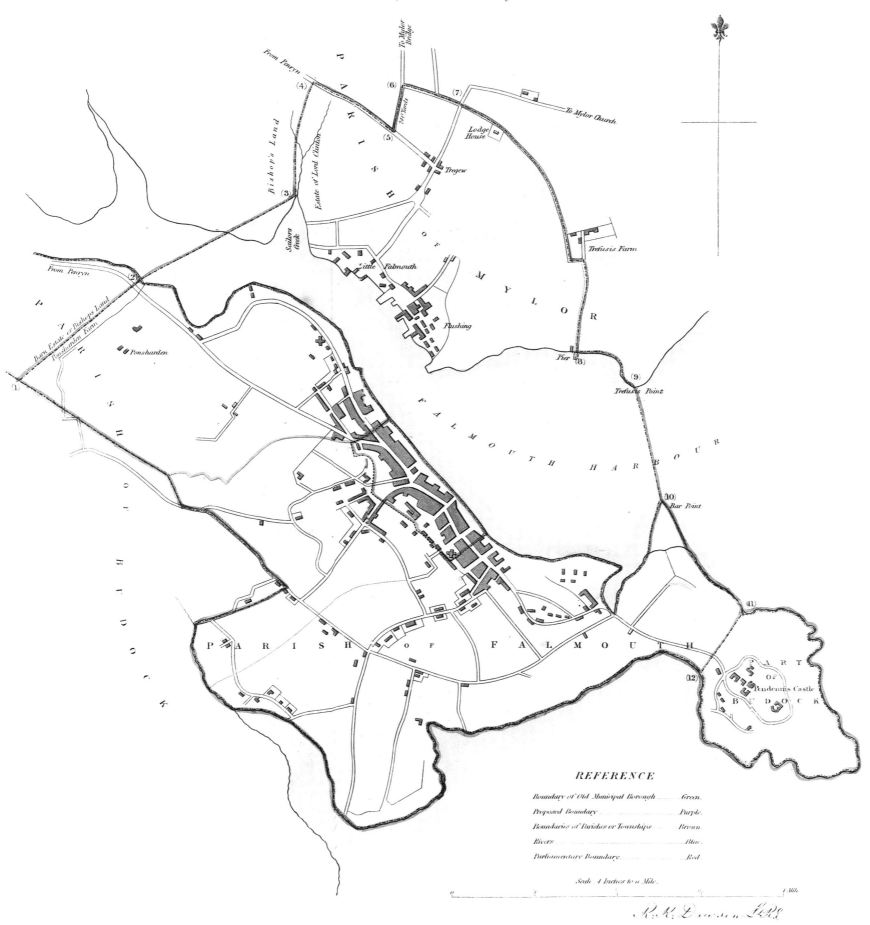

REFERENCE

Boundary of Old Municipal Borough	Green.
Proposed Boundary	Purple.
Boundaries of Parishes or Townships	Brown.
Rivers	Blue.
Parliamentary Boundary	Red.

Scale 4 Inches to a Mile.

Aberystwyth

Plan of Aberystwyth, Cardigan, by John Wood 1834. Aberystwyth is situated 208 miles from London, and has a population of 4,128. A market town and sea-port Aberystwyth is situated at the confluence of the Rivers Ystwith and Rhyddol, where the former falls into the sea in the bay of Cardigan.

It is seated on a craggy eminence which projects into the sea, and commands a magnificent view of the whole line of the Welsh coast within Cardigan Bay. The streets are steep and uneven, and the houses, being chiefly formed of dark slate, present a very singular appearance. For some years past, its celebrity, as a summer retreat and bathing place, has been annually increasing, to which the beauty of the neighbourhood, and the commanding prospects all around, very greatly contribute. The roads to it have been made excellent, and the usual amusements of plays, and assemblies during the season, increase its attractions for summer visitants. There was formerly a herring fishery on the coast, and fishing is still pursued with considerable advantage by the natives of the town.

Fairs are held in May and November, chiefly for the hiring of servants.

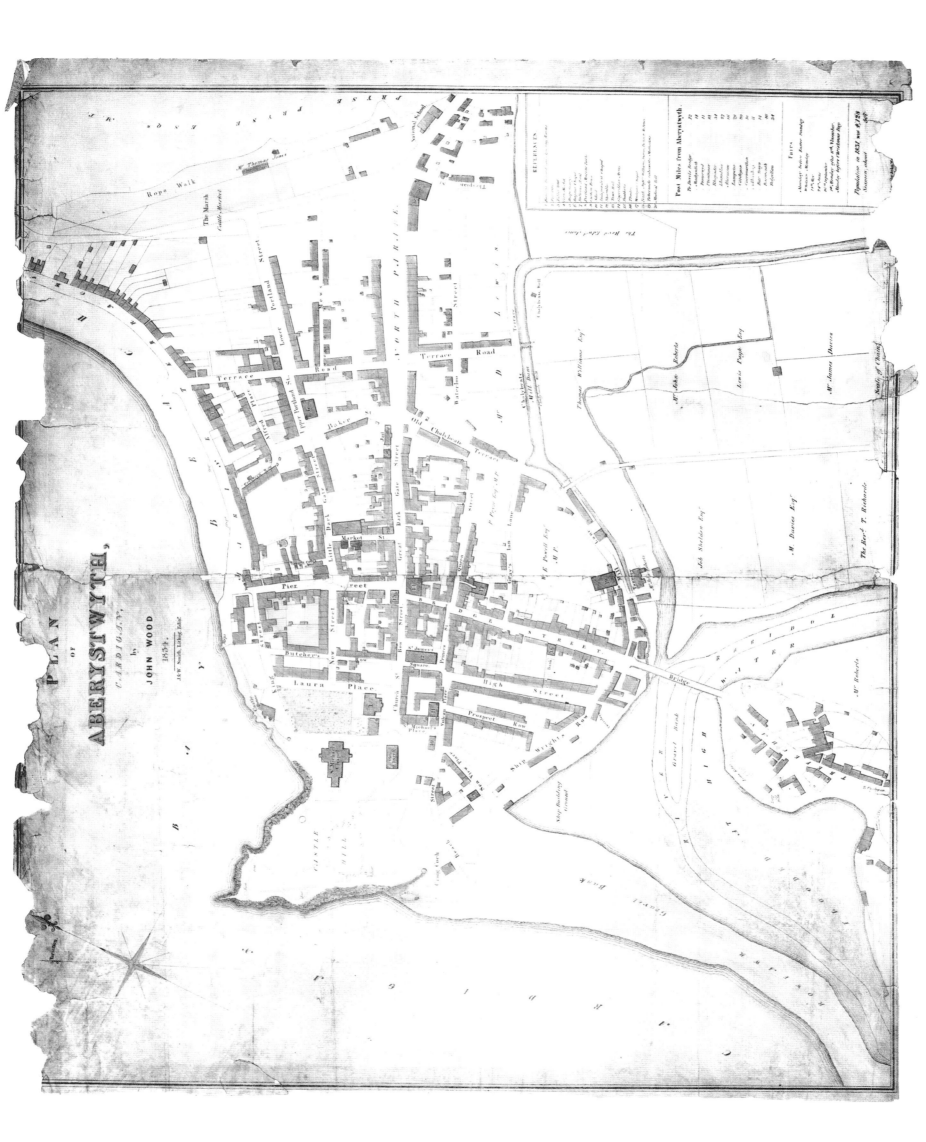

PLAN
OF
ABERYSTWYTH,
CARDIGAN,
by
JOHN WOOD
1834.
J&W Smith, Lithog Edinr.

Bangor

Plan of Bangor, from Actual Survey by John Wood 1834. The city of Bangor is situated 236 miles from London and has a population of 4,750.

Bangor lies at the foot of a steep rock, in a narrow and fertile vale, near the northern entrance to the Menai Strait. It consists of one principal street, nearly a mile in length, and much too narrow for so great a thoroughfare, with several smaller avenues opening into it from the water side. Since the construction of that admirable work of art, the Menai Bridge, Bangor has risen into some importance, being visited by upwards of 50,000 persons annually, who remain for longer or shorter periods. Houses are regularly prepared for the reception of lodgers in the summer season. Many neat villas have been erected in the vicinity; and the spacious inn, built by Mr Pennant, affords elegant accommodation for one hundred inmates at a time. Its proximity to the sea has given Bangor the advantage of becoming a favourite bathing-place; and the views of Beaumaris Bay and the Caernarvon mountains from Garth Point, the promenade of the inhabitants, are of the most pictures-que, bold, and sublime character. The principal public buildings are the cathedral, the bishop's palace, free school, market house and three excellent inns.

The trade of this place consists entirely in the export of slates raised in the quarries of Llandegai, seven miles from the town, and conveyed on a railway to Port Penrhyn, where there is an excellent and convenient quay. A castle is now in progress of erection within the demesne of Mr Pennant adjacent to the city, on the site of the palace of Roderic, Prince of Wales in 720, on a scale of great extent and magnificence. It is built in the pure Saxon style of architecture, at an expense perhaps exceeding £100,000.

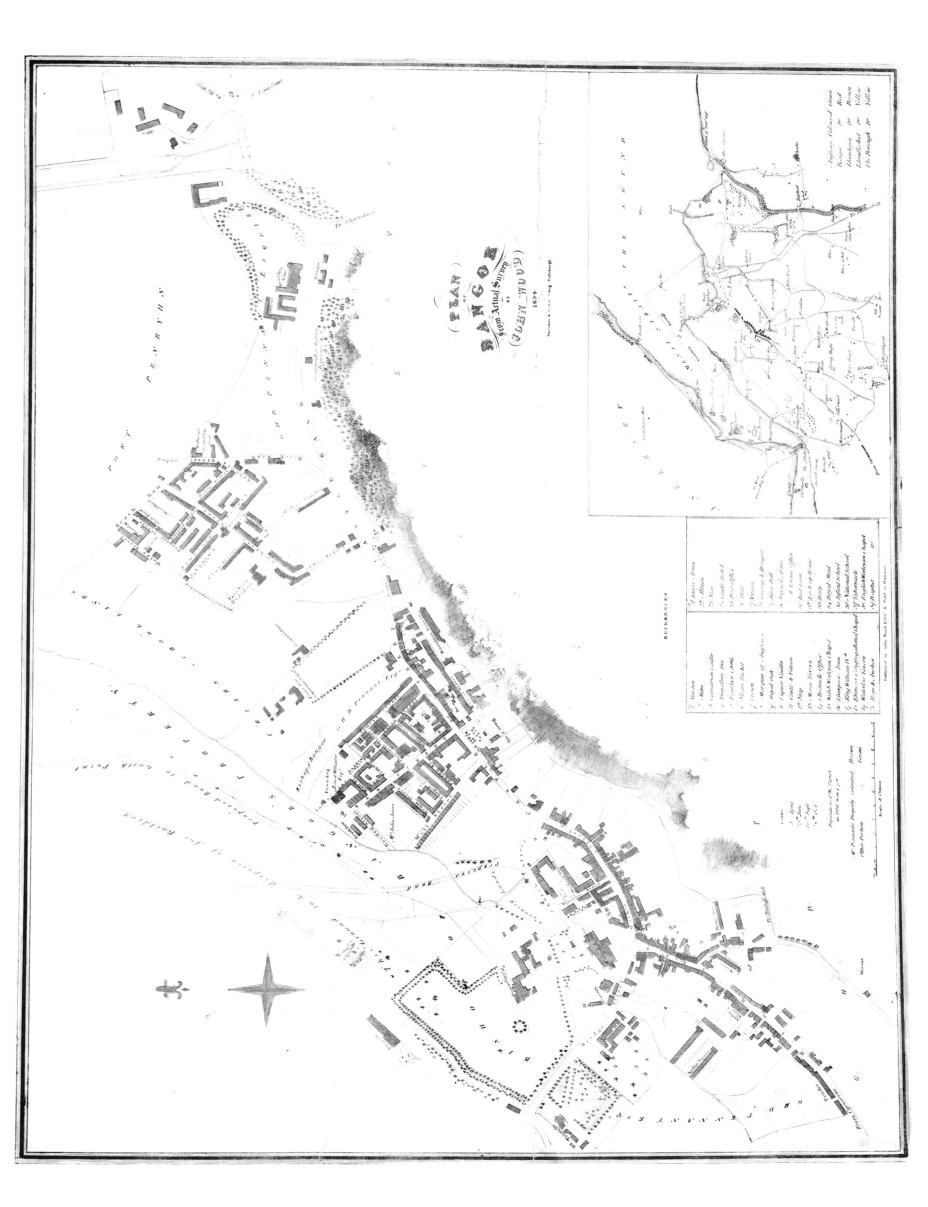

PLAN
OF
BANGOR
From Actual Survey
BY
JOHN WOOD
1834

Forrester & Nichol, Lithog. Edinburgh

REFERENCES.

1. Auction
2. Mint
3. Carnarvon Castle
4. Travellers Inn
5. Cruckes Castle
6. Slanes Packet
7. Crown
8. Marquis of Anglesea
9. Royal Oak
10. Engine Cradle
11. Castle & Falcon
12. Ship
13. Mona Tavern
14. Chronicle Office
15. Welsh Wesleyan Chapel
16. Liverpool Arms
17. King William IVth
18. Ebenezer Congregational Chapel
19. Waterloo Tavern
20. Hope & Anchor
21. Princes Arms
22. Union
23. Star
24. Castle Hotel
25. Post Office
26. Bull
27. Wheat
28. George & Dragon
29. White Hall
30. Reynolds Arms
31. Excise Office
32. Red Lion
33. Lock up House
34. Harp
35. Royal Mail
36. Infant School
37. National School
38. Fishermaid
39. English Wesleyan Chapel
40. Penrhyn Arms

Scale of Chains

Population of the Parish
in 1834 was 7,700

Mr Pennants Property coloured Brown
Other Portion   Green

Published by John Wood Edinr & Sold at Bangor

Caernarvon

Plan of the town of Caernarvon from actual survey by John Wood 1834. Caernarvon is 235 miles from London, and has a population of 7,752.

Caernarvon is beautifully situated on the Straits of Menai, and is entirely surrounded by its magnificent castle and walls, with towers at short intervals. The town, within the walls, consists of 10 streets, the chief of which is High Street, running from the land to the water-gates, and consisting principally of shops, many of which for elegance and convenience may vie with those of any town in England. The town without the walls consisted of 18 streets, the best of which is on the Bangor and Pwllheli roads; but several new ones have recently been built, together with several handsome villas in different parts of the suburbs.

There is a beautiful terrace without the wall of the town, forming the principal promenade of the inhabitants, the prospects from which are most extensive and delightful. At the north end of the terrace, a new pier is now constructing, which, when finished, will extend a mile into the river. At the south end of the terrace is the custom-house, from which the quay extends along the banks of the River Seiont under the walls of the castle. Edward I walled the modern town in 1282, and erected this princely castle, deemed one of the finest of its kind in Europe, and yet which is externally perfect.

Caernarvon has no manufactures. The principal exports are slate and copper ore, of the former of which several hundred thousand are exported to all parts of Europe and America. The pleasant situation of this town, its facilities for bathing, and the cheapness and plenty of its markets have greatly increased the number of residents in recent years. At the back of the town is a hill called Twt Hill, which commands a most varied and extensive prospect of mountain, hill, dale, and ocean. The harbour is tolerably good, with 9 feet at low water.

[Author's note: despite the claim made for it, the inset plan of Caernarvon does not date from the reign of Henry VIII. It is however, the earliest known plan of the city, on John Speed's map of the county, from the *Theatre of the Empire of Great Britaine*, which was published in 1612.]

PLAN
(OF THE TOWN OF)
(CAERNARVON)
FROM ACTUAL SURVEY
by John Wood
1834

REFERENCES
N° 1 Uxbridge Arms Hotel
2 Fish Market
3 Independent Chapel
4 S.ᵗ Marys D°
5 Baths
6 Bank Mess.ʳˢ Williams & C°
7 Shambles
8 Guild Hall
9 Commercial Inn
b Post Office
10 Sportsman Hotel
11 Corn Market formerly Plas Mawr
12 Crown & Anchor
13 The Harp
14 Calvinistic Methodist Chapel
15 Jail
16 Custom House
17 County Hall
18 Goat Hotel
19 Castle D°
20 English Wesleyan Chapel
21 Welsh D° D°
22 Baptist D°
23 National Schools
C Plas Puleston
d Plas Spicer
e Plas Bowman
f Llanberis & Drws y Coed Copper Ore Yard
K Smidde Dyllvan C° D°

Population of the Parish
in 1831 was 7752
Population of the Town 6252

POST MILES FROM CAERNARVON
T. Bangor .... 9 Miles
Menai Bridge 8
Beaumaris 15
Mona Inn 18
Delbadarn Foot of Snowdon 8
Lakes & Slate Quarries .. 10
Llanberis Village 10
Bettws 6
Snowdon Guide House .. 8
Beddgelert 13
Tremadoc 20
Clynnog 10
Pwllheli 20

FAIRS
March 1.ᵗ &
May 16.ᵗ &
August 1.ˢᵗ &
September 5.ᵗ &
December 9.ᵗ &
Market day Saturday

This Plan was drawn in the Reign of Henry the Eighth, in the year 1520 & found in the possession of W.B. Jones Caernarvon.

Cardigan

Plan of Cardigan from an Actual Survey 1834. Cardigan is 239 miles from London. The population in 1831 was 2,795, mariners not included.

Cardigan occupies a steep hill and consists of two principal streets, containing many respectable houses. The River Teifi is crossed by a handsome stone bridge of seven arches. The church is ancient, but adorned by a beautiful tower, rising from the western end; the town-hall and poor-house are only half a century old. The remains of the castle, which are inconsiderable, consist of two round towers, connected by a curtain-wall, mantled with ivy, and presenting a venerable appearance.

Here are no manufactures, but a coasting-trade, which employs about 300 bottoms and upwards of 1,000 mariners. The coracle, a species of boat, anciently much used in Ireland and Wales, continues to be employed on the river in this town.

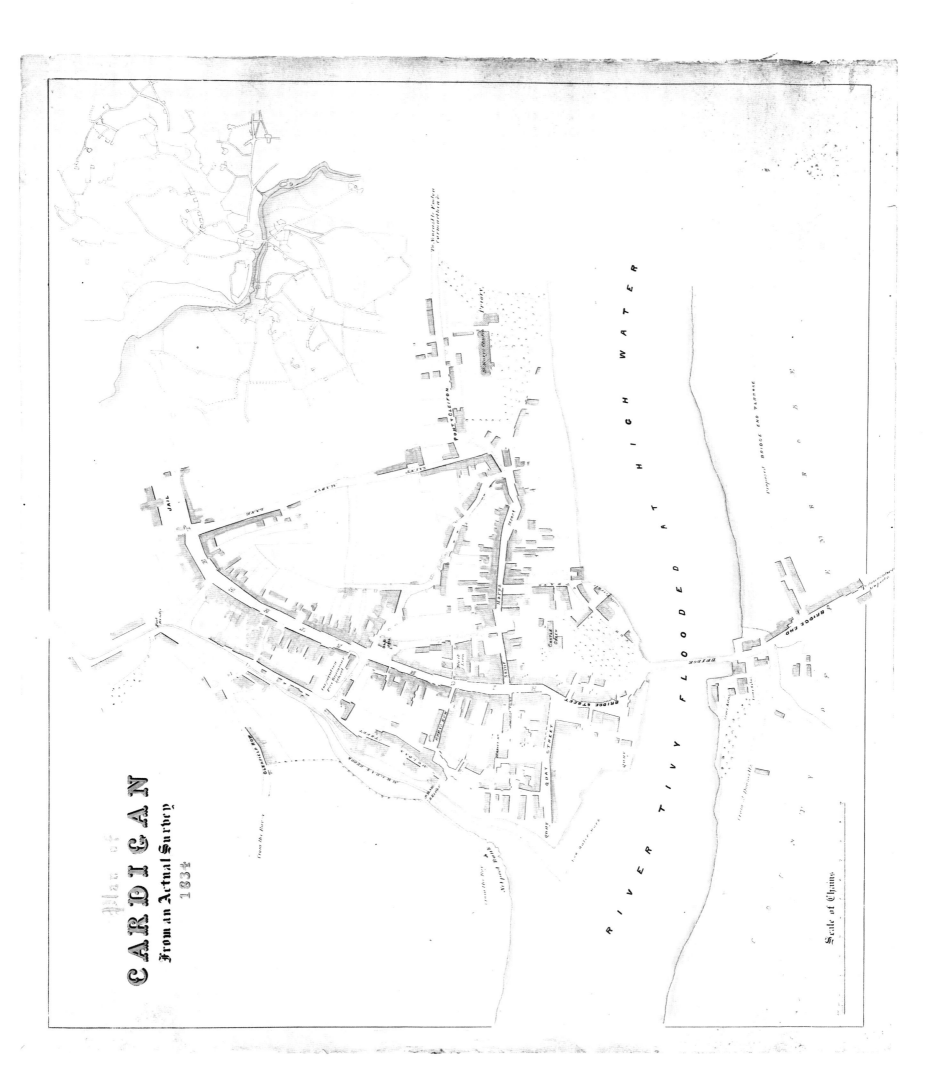

Plan of
CARDIGAN
From an Actual Survey
1834

Scale of Chains

JOHN TALLIS

Aberdeen

Aberdeen is 122 miles from Edinburgh, and has a population of 64,778. The chief city of the north of Scotland, it is situated near the discharge of the Dee into the German Ocean, on ground rising into a gentle slope from the sea. Aberdeen is a large and handsome town, the principal streets being spacious, with rows of lofty houses, constructed with granite from the neighbouring quarries. In the centre is the market-place, an oblong square, of considerable dimensions, on the north side of which stand the town house and prison, each surmounted with a spire. Two remarkably fine streets form the entrances from the north and south, the latter of which, called Union Street, passes over a deep ravine, by an extended arch of cut granite. The harbour, which at one time was very dangerous owing to the frequent shifting of a bar of sand, is now rendered safe by a noble pier on the north side of the river, constructed of granite, after a plan by the celebrated engineer Smeaton.

The inhabitants of this city carry on a very considerable business, both in trade and manufacture. The latter include cotton, linen, and woollen, in their various branches, but more particularly, brown linen, canvas, sail-cloth, sheeting, hosiery, carpeting, coarse yarn, bleached and coloured thread, with nails, cordage, and most of the articles connected with ship-building, which is also much pursued. The foreign trade is principally carried on with North America, the West Indies, the Mediterranean and the Baltic; the imports being chiefly from the latter. The articles exported are grain, meal, thread, hosiery, cotton and linen goods, salmon, pickled pork, and granite to London. Of exported salmon, the fisheries on the Don and the Dee annually supply an average of 2,000 barrels.

The city has long been celebrated as a seat of learning, by possessing the Marischal College and Univeristy, founded by George, Earl Marischal, in 1530.

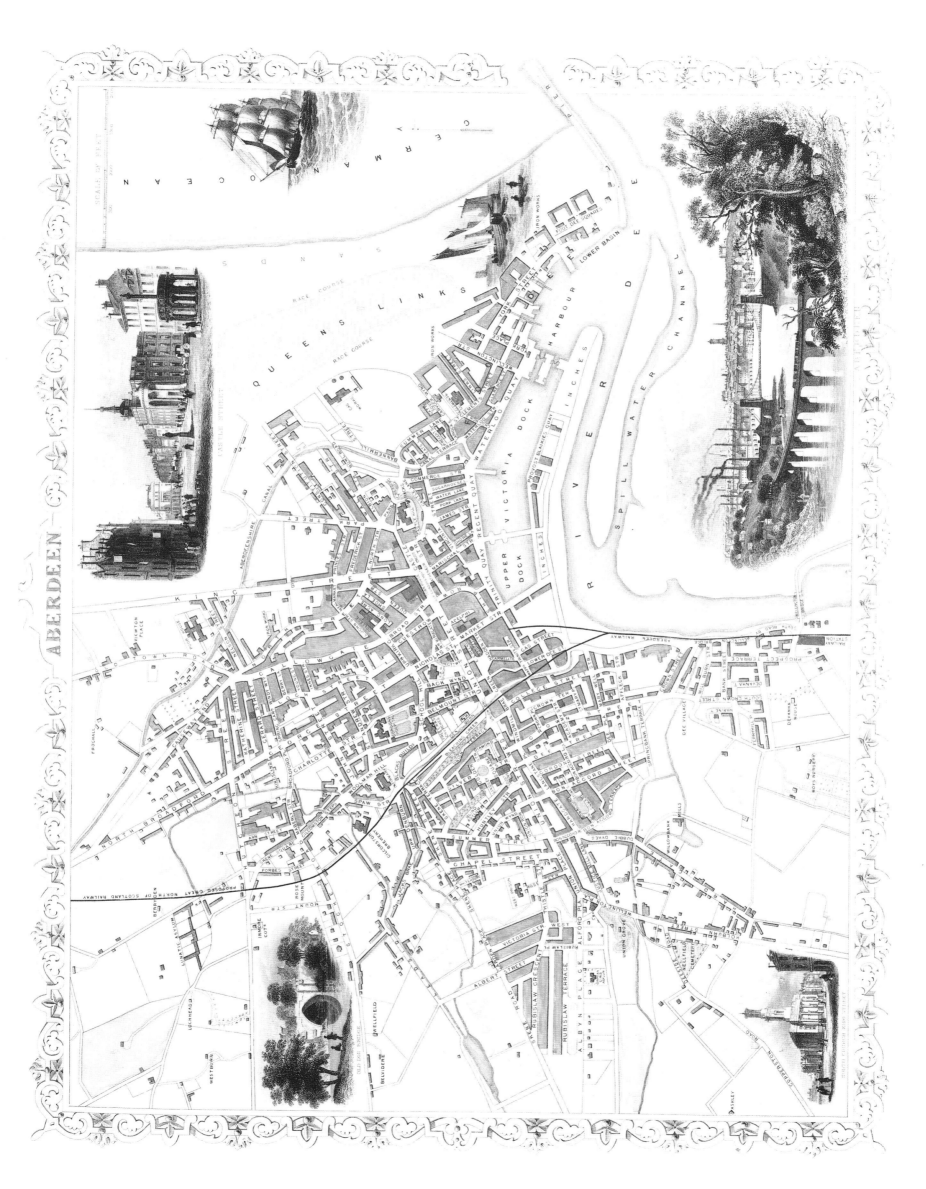

ABERDEEN

GERMAN OCEAN

SANDS

QUEENS LINKS

RACE COURSE

RACE COURSE

RIVER DEE

SPILL WATER CHANNEL

HARBOUR

Lower Basin

Dock
Victoria Dock
Waterloo Quay
Regent Quay
Upper Dock
Trinity Quay
Market Str
Inches

KING STREET

CASTLE STREET

Aberdeenshire Canal

NORTH BROADFORD

UNION STREET

ABERDEEN RAILWAY

PROPOSED GREAT NORTH OF SCOTLAND RAILWAY

RAILWAY STATION

PROSPECT TERRACE

DEE VILLAGE

DEVANNA HOUSE

LUNATIC ASYLUM

WESTBURN

WELLFIELD

BELVIDERE

CHAPEL STREET

ALBYN PLACE
ALFORD PLACE
RUBISLAW TERRACE

VICTORIA STR
ALBERT STREET

UNION GROVE

NELLFIELD CEMETERY

DEESIDE ROAD

Belfast

Belfast is 80 miles from Dublin, and has a population of 75,308. The town is advantageously situated on the western bank of the River Lagan. Its general appearance is cheerful and prepossessing; the principal streets and squares, which are well formed and spacious, are macadamized, and the footpaths flagged with excellent freestone. Though situated little more than six feet above high water mark of spring tides, the town is considered healthy, the air being pure and salubrious; and the surrounding scenery is richly diversified and, in many parts, picturesque.

Belfast owes much of its importance to the increase of the linen trade of Ulster, of which it is now become the grand depot. The business of the linen trade was for a long time conducted solely in Dublin, but in 1785 a spacious and handsome quadrangular building was erected in the centre of Donegal Square and called the White Linen Hall, which affords great facility for making up assorted cargoes for foreign countries. Belfast is also the centre and principal seat of the cotton manufacture; the principal articles manufactured are velvets, fustians, jeans, ticking, checks, ginghams, quiltings, calico muslins and muslinettes. There are twelve extensive ale and porter breweries, from which many thousand barrels are exported; some large flour and meal mills; and extensive manufactories for tobacco, soap, candles, starch, glue and paper.

The port is very advantageously situated for trade at the mouth of Belfast Lough; the preservation and improvement of the port and harbour are vested in the Ballast Corporation. There are in Smithfield two market places for meat, two for fish, and one for hay, straw and hides, besides several others for meat and vegetables in various parts of the town, all of which are well supplied.

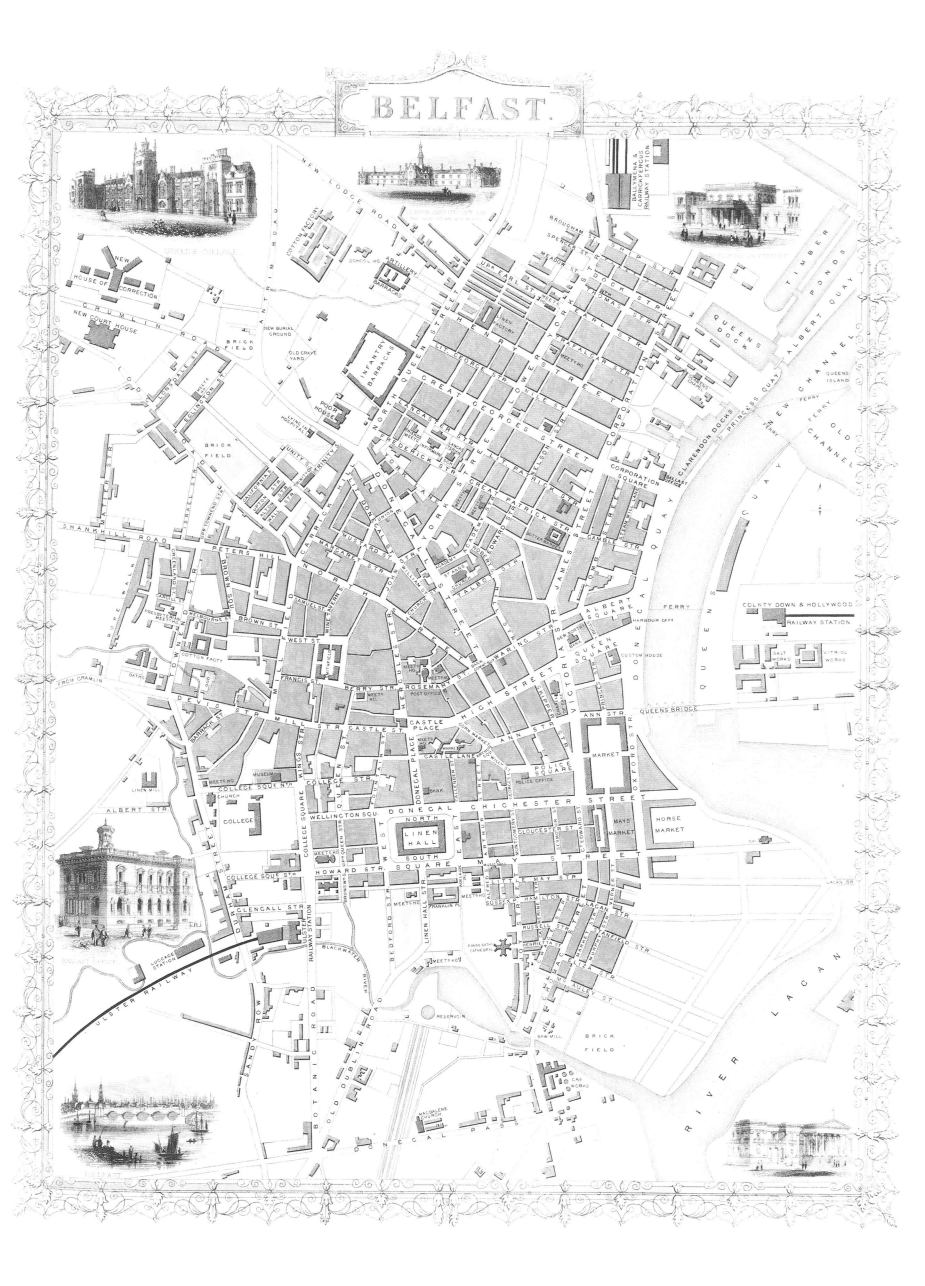

BELFAST.

QUEEN'S COLLEGE

BALLYMENA & CARRICKFERGUS RAILWAY STATION

NEW LODGE ROAD

ANTRIM ROAD

COTTON FACTORY

SCHOOL HO

ARTILLERY BARRACKS

NEW HOUSE OF CORRECTION

CRUMLIN ROAD

NEW COURT HOUSE

NEW BURIAL GROUND

OLD GRAVE YARD

BRICK FIELD

INFANTRY BARRACKS

POOR HOUSE

LYING IN HOSPITAL

BROUGHAM ST

SPENCER ST

MEADOW ST

DOCK

THOMAS ST

UPR EARL ST

HENRY ST

LINEN FACTORY

LIT GEORGE STR

TRAFALGAR STREET

CREAT GEORGES STR

LOWER GEORGES STREET

CORPORATION ST

QUEENS DOCK

TIMBER PONDS

ALBERT QUAY

NEW CHANNEL

QUEENS ISLAND

QUEENS CHAPEL

FERRY

FERRY

OLD CHANNEL

BRICK FIELD

LONSDALE STR

ECLINTON ST

TRINITY ST

TRINITY ST

CALIFORNIA

UPR TOWNSEND STR

UNION

FREDERICK STR

DONEGALL ST

YORK STREET

PATRICK STR

PATRICK STR

CLARENDON DOCKS

PRINCES ST

PRINCESS QUAY

BALLAST OFFICE

SHANKHILL ROAD

ISRAEL STR

PETERS HILL

GREENLAND

BROWN SQ

CARRICK HILL

NORTH QUEEN STREET

CHURCH STR

ACADEMY STR

TOMB STREET

JAMES STREET

CORPORATION ST

CAMBLE STR

TEAM MILL LANE

BUTTER

HARBOUR OFF

CUSTOM HOUSE

FERRY

QUEENS QUAY

COUNTY DOWN & HOLLYWOOD RAILWAY STATION

FROM CRAMLIN

ROPE WALK

TOWNSEND

COTTON FACTY

BATHS

PRESBYTERIAN MEETING

CARRIC ST

MELBOURNE ST

BROWN ST

MILLFIELD

SAMUEL STREET

WINE TAVERN S

SMITHFIELD

NORTH

CHURCH

LANE

TALBOT

DONEGALL STREET

ROBERT STR

ST ANN

WARING STREET

SHIPPER STR

ALBERT SQUARE

NEW NORTH

QUEEN SQUARE

VICTORIA STREET

PRINCE STR

SALT WORKS

VITRIOL WORKS

DEVIS STR

MILL STR

WEST ST

FRANCIS ST

BERRY STR

ROSEMARY

MEETG HO

MEETG

POST OFFICE

HERCULES STR

HIGH STREET

ANN STR

ANN STREET

POLICE SQUARE

MARKET

QUEENS BRIDGE

BARRACK STR

MUSEUM

CASTLE ST

CASTLE PLACE

DONEGAL PLACE

CORN MARKET

CASTLE LANE

WILLS

BANK

POLICE OFFICE

HORSE MARKET

MEETG HO

COLLEGE SQUN NTH

COLLEGE STR

QUEEN STR

WELLINGTON SQU

KINGS STR

DONEGAL

CHICHESTER STREET

OXFORD STR

MAYS MARKET

LINEN MILL

CHURCH

COLLEGE

COLLEGE SQUE STH

HOWARD STR

DONEGAL SQUARE

NORTH LINEN HALL SOUTH

GLOUCESTER ST

EDWARD STR

ALBERT STR

HAMILTON STR

BRUNSW

QUEEN STR

BEDFORD STR

LINEN HALL STR

ARTHUR STR

MAY

MUSIC HALL

MEETG HO

FRANKLIN PL

SUSSEX

ALFRED

LITTLE MAY ST

VERNER ST

HAMILTON STR

LAGAN ST

VERNER

RUSSELL STR

MARKET STR

CROMAC ST

PANFIELD STR

ELIZA

HENRIETTA STR

BALLAST OFFICE

DUNCAIRN STR

HAMILTON STR

GLENGALL STR

BLACKWATER

ULSTER RAILWAY STATION

ROMAN CATH CATHEDRAL

MEETG HO

MC AULEY ST

LUCGAGE STATION

ULSTER RAILWAY

SANDY ROW

BOTANIC ROAD

OLD DUBLIN ROAD

RIVER LACAN

RESERVOIR

SAW MILL

BRICK FIELD

RIVER LAGAN

LACAN BR

MACDALENE CHURCH

DONEGAL PASS

CAS WORKS

BELFAST

Bradford

Bradford lies 196 miles from London; its population is 105,207. The town stands at the junction of three fine valleys, amid a diversified, picturesque, hilly country, within the basin of the River Aire. A canal goes from its centre to the Leeds and Liverpool Canal, leading the way to the German Ocean and the Irish Sea; and branch railways go northward, eastward, and southward, passing speedily into railway lines which ramify towards all parts of the kingdom.

The town is chiefly built of fine freestone and contains many very handsome edifices, both private and public. It includes narrow, ill-constructed streets, but has recently undergone great improvement. It is extending in all directions; and it possesses such suburbs or goes so nearly into adjacent villages, as to be practically a town for miles. It looks from the neighbourhood to be full of factories; the town contains some of the finest warehouses in the kingdom.

St George's Hall, in the centre of the town, covers an area of 1,600 yards, and was erected in 1851–3 at a cost of £13,000.

Manufactures of worsted yarn and worsted stuffs have long been carried on; manufactures of damask, moreen, and mixed worsted and silk goods are now extensive. Manufactures of cotton fabrics engage attention; and extensive ironworks, together with abundant supplies of iron-ore and coal.

The places of worship in 1851 were 32 of the Church of England; 1 of the United Presbyterian Church; 17 of Independents; 15 of Baptists; 1 of Quakers; 2 of Unitarians; 3 of Moravians; 43 of Wesleyan Methodists; 3 of New Connexion Methodists; 18 of Primitive Methodists; 5 of the Wesleyan Association; 10 of Wesleyan Reformers; 5 undefined; 3 of Latter Day Saints; 1 of Catholics.

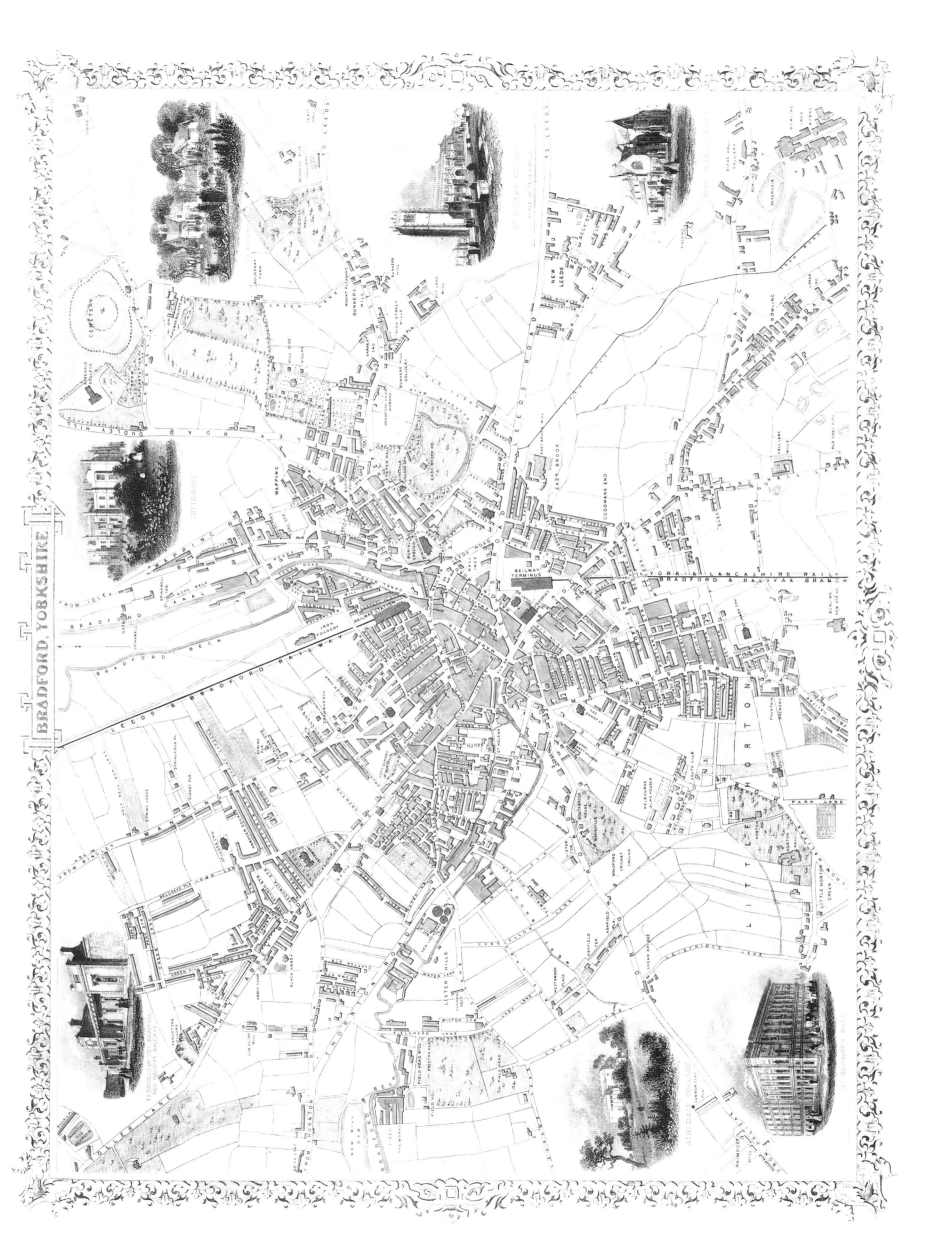

BRADFORD, YORKSHIRE

JOHN TALLIS

Brighton

Brighton is 50 miles from London, its population is 48,567. The town stands on a swell, slope, and cliff under the South Downs. The sea before it forms a great slender bay surrounded by Beachy Head and Selsey Bill. One railway goes direct to London; another goes to Lewes and thence to Kent; and a third goes to Chichester and Portsmouth, and thence to the west. Anciently the name was Brighthelmstone, and continues so in all legal and parochial documents.

Brighton went into decline till about 1750; and had then only about 800 inhabitants, chiefly poor fishermen. Dr Russell, a distinguished physician, drew attention to it, as a desirable bathing place; and some persons of influence and fashion soon began to visit it from London. Dr Johnson was here in 1770; and the Prince of Wales, afterwards George IV, first came in 1782, and then founded a permanent residence in 1784. Brighton suddenly underwent a change of fortune, and it has gone on increasing, steadily and rapidly, from that time to the present, so as to be now the greatest watering place in the world.

The town extends three miles from Hove to Kemp Town and presents such an imposing frontage to the sea as cannot be rivalled by any other town. All of it, with small exception, is modern; and much is handsome, elegant or grand. The central position includes the Steyne named from the Staine or Rock on which the fishermen of the old town used to dry their nets; the Pavilion or Palace built by George IV and two large enclosures that are thickly planted with shrubs.

The western portion includes the early fashionable extensions, exhibits a prevailing character of comparative stiffness or uniformity; and contains the fine localities of Regency Square, Brunswick Square and Adelaide Crescent.

The eastern portion includes the later extensions; here, Kemp Town was commenced in 1831, on the estate of Thomas Read Kemp.

The Pavilion of George IV underwent additions and changes until 1817; assumed a fantastic character, with domes, minarets, cupolas, and spires, alleged to resemble the Kremlin at Moscow; and was sold in 1850 to the local authorities for £53,000.

The climate differs as to warmth, in the higher and lower parts, and in the east and west; but, on the whole, is of comparatively brisk dry character, excellent for children and healthy adults, and suitable for invalids of well-toned constitution.

Manufactures and commerce are little more than nominal, while the retail trade of the town is extensive.

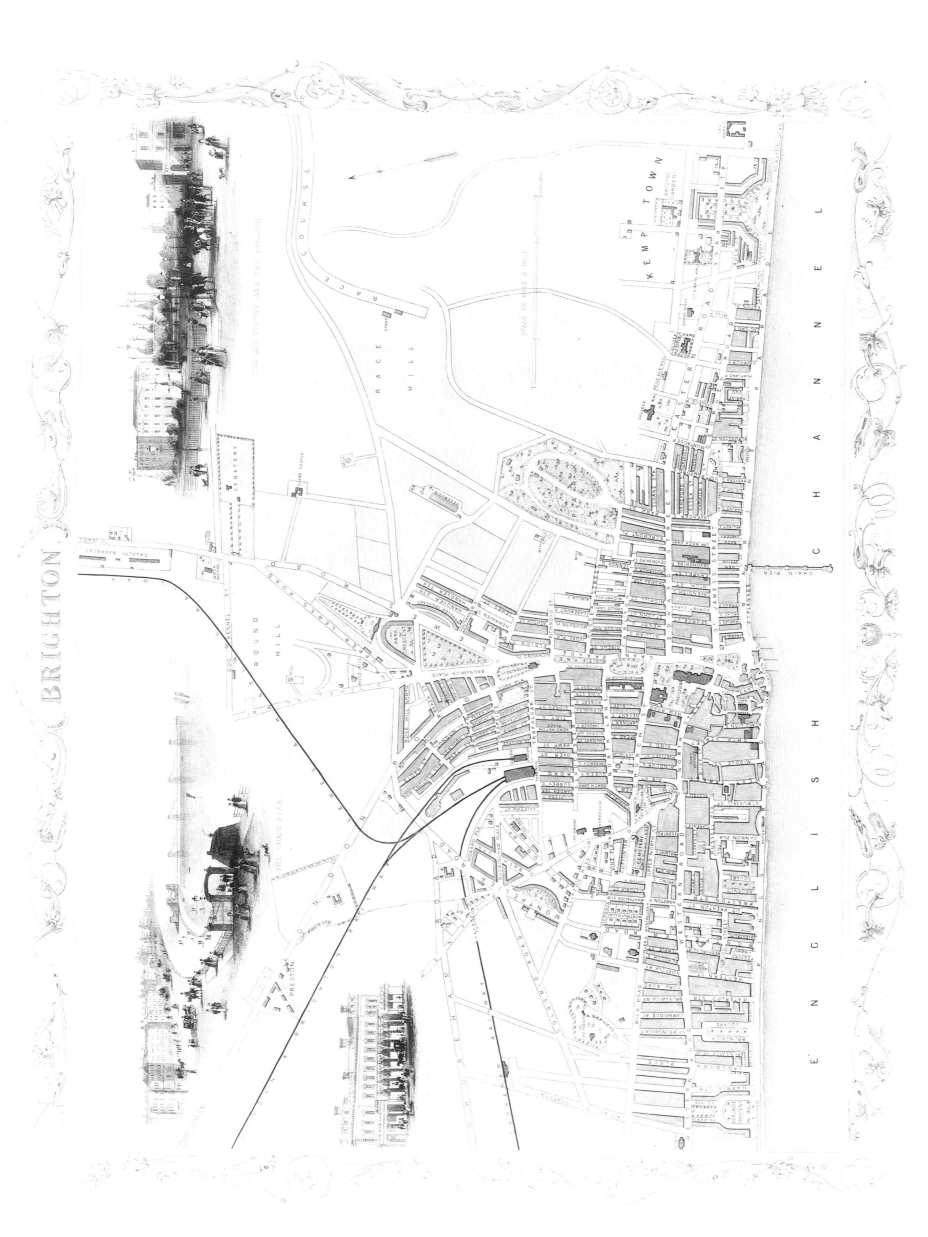

BRIGHTON.

JOHN TALLIS

Clifton and Bristol

Bristol, 118 miles from London, has a population of 123,188 and is positioned on the mutual border of Gloucester and Somerset. It stands on the River Avon, at the influx of the Frome, 6 miles in direct distance from the Avon's mouth. The Avon has a tidal rise at it of nearly 30 feet; was partly diverted past Bristol in a new deep cut in 1804–9, with the formation of a great floating harbour; and gives it, for large sea-home vessels, all the characters of a sea-port.

The site of Bristol is diversified in both form and elevation. Some of it consists of eminences, rising high above the level of the neighbouring streets, and much is a variety of slope, declining chiefly to the Avon. The city-proper, or ancient city, is on the right bank of the river, intersected by long and ramified reaches of the floating harbour. The Clifton suburb, itself almost a city, is on the same bank, further down, but almost conjoined with the city-proper by recent buildings; and the Bedminster suburb is on the left bank, separated from the ancient city only by the river.

The ancient city shows more resemblance than perhaps any other place in Britain with some of the old towns of Belgium and Germany. Some of the streets are very narrow; lanes, courts, and alleys are numerous; and many of the houses are curious ancient structures, with overhanging upper stories, numerous windows, and front gables; but these interesting relics are now disappearing under modern improvements. The central point is at the intersection of High-street from the south-east, Broad-street from the north-west, Corn-street from the south-west, and Wine-street from the north-east. One of the most striking of the picturesque old thoroughfares is Maryport-street, opening into High-street. The more modern parts of the city, on all sides of the ancient one, contain many spacious streets, many of them well aligned, and some parts are distinguished by elegant houses.

A riot, of three days' continuance, occurred in 1831, involved a destruction of property to the value of about £70,000, and occasioned wounds or death to several hundred individuals. Among the buildings damaged or destroyed were the Bishop's palace, the Custom-house, re-erected on the same site, the Excise Office, the Bridewell, afterwards rebuilt in larger and better form on the same site, and the jail.

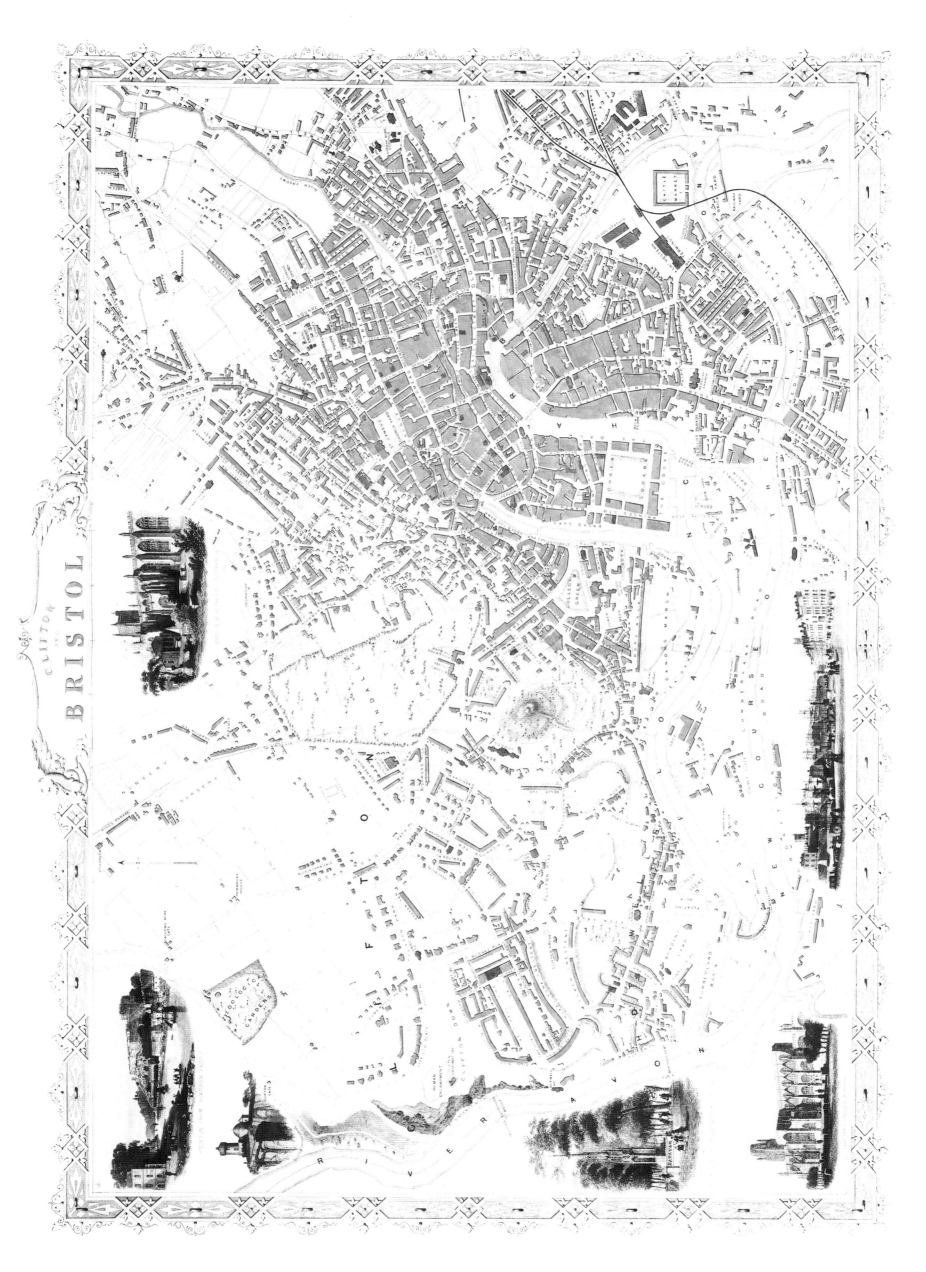

BRISTOL

CLIFTON AND

Cork

Cork is 126 miles from Dublin, with a population of 106,055. This place, which in extent and importance is the second city in Ireland, is distinguished for its fine harbour, and its situation on the navigable River Lee. One mile west of the cathedral the River Lee divides into two branches, insulating a tract about two miles in length and half a mile in breadth, on which the ancient city was built; and uniting again at its eastern extremity, expands into a noble estuary a mile broad, forming the commencement of the harbour. The rapid advancement of the city may be attributed to the great capabilities of its almost matchless haven which renders it the emporium of commerce for this part of the country, so spacious and deep, as to be capable of containing the largest vessels, and the most extensive fleets. The general appearance of the city is picturesque and cheerful; most of the houses are large and well built, chiefly of clay-slate, fronted with roofing slate, which gives them a clean, though sombre, appearance.

The butter trade is considered as the most important in the province of Munster, and is carried on in this city to a greater extent that in any other city in the United Kingdom. The introduction of steam navigation has much increased the exportation of flour to London, Liverpool, and Bristol; while the trade in livestock, in poultry and eggs, and produce of the river fisheries, has been greatly promoted and is now very extensive. On an average, 1,200 pigs and half a million eggs are sent off weekly.

The noted castle of Blarney, five miles from Cork, was built in 1446, by Cormack McCarthy, but is now a picturesque ruin. The interest which both natives and strangers take in the castle arises more from a tradition connected with a stone in its north-eastern angle, then from any other circumstance; this is called 'the Blarney stone' in reference to a notion that, if anyone kisses it, he will ever after have a cajoling tongue and the art of flattery or of telling lies with unblushing effrontery.

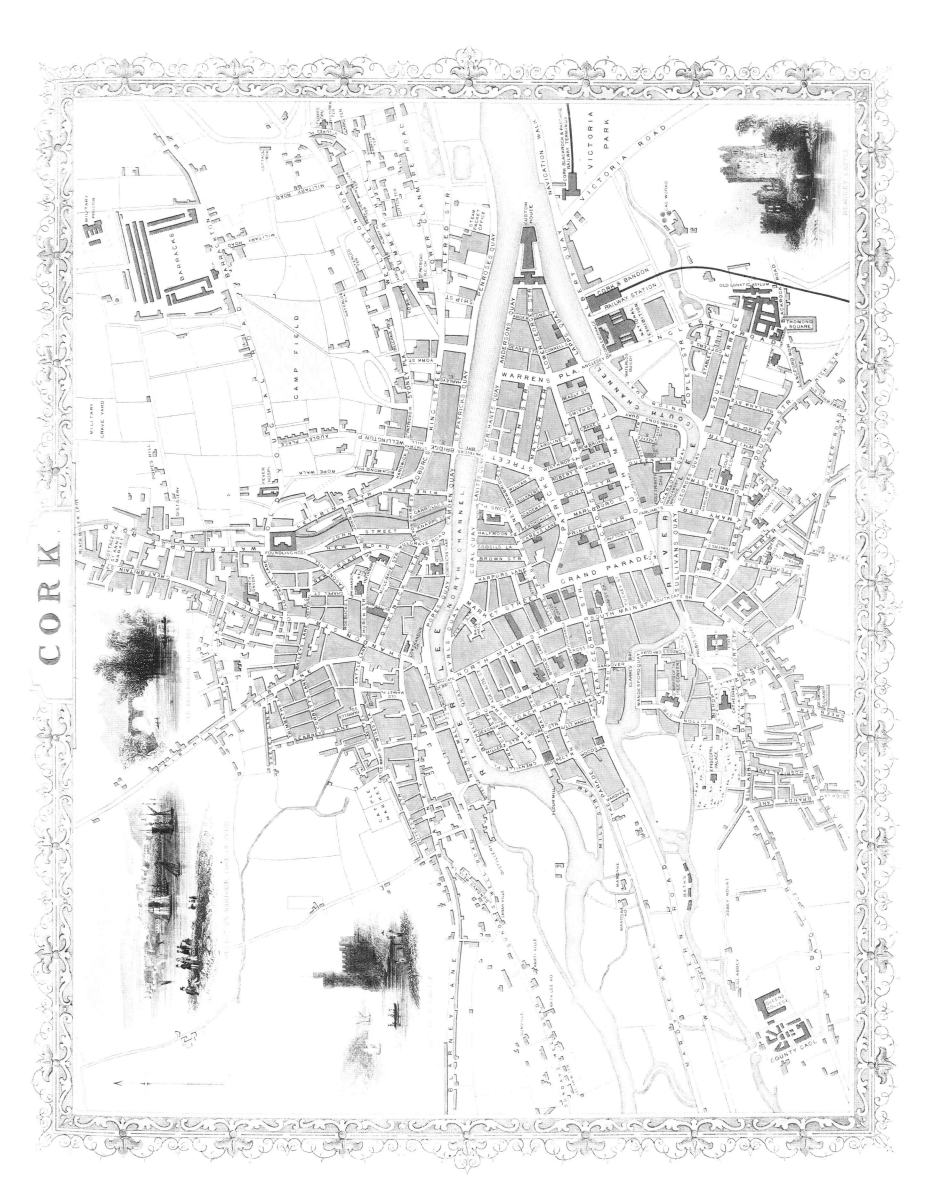

CORK.

Exeter

Exeter is 171 miles south-west of London, its population is 31,312. By railway, Exeter is 39½ miles south-east of Barnstable, 52¾ north-east by east of Plymouth, 75½ south-west of Bristol, 169½ south-west of Birmingham, and 194 west-south-west of London; and has railway communication in three directions, towards Plymouth, Barnstable, Bristol and London, with such numerous ramifications, either completed or in progress, as connect it with all parts of the kingdom.

Exeter was a town of the ancient Britons long before the Roman Invasion; and it has made a conspicuous figure in every subsequent age. The city occupies the slopes and summit of a flat ridge, rising to the height of about 150 feet from the left bank of the Exe. The ridge ascends gradually on one side, descends abruptly on the other, and is engirt with rich undulating country. The city-proper, or the old city, or the part within the circuit of the ancient walls, covers a space of about ½ mile by 3 furlongs, nearly in the form of a parallelogram; and is intersected, in a cruciform manner, by four principal streets, which meet at right angles near the centre. The suburbs are of various character, and have various expansions; but, on the whole, they include many old streets, and a number of new fine thoroughfares and squares. The principal streets, in all parts of the city, both old and new, are spacious; and some of the recently erected places are at once airy and elegant; yet many of the streets, especially the older ones, are narrow. High-street is very cheerful, and contains handsome shops, and many curious old shop-fronts.

Numerous parts show features of antiquity; while most parts, especially the modern streets, and the handsome squares and terraces, present a highly pleasing aspect, and indicate a prosperous and tasteful care for renovation, embellishment and extension. So large a sum as upwards of £70,000 was recently expended in drainage, in ventilating over-crowded places, by the removal of houses and the widening of streets, and in other kindred improvements. The city altogether, from the conjoint effects of its site, structure, and its police arrangements, is one of the cleanest, and most orderly, and best regulated in the kingdom; and at the same time, from the purity, mildness, and equability of its climate, is one of the most healthy.

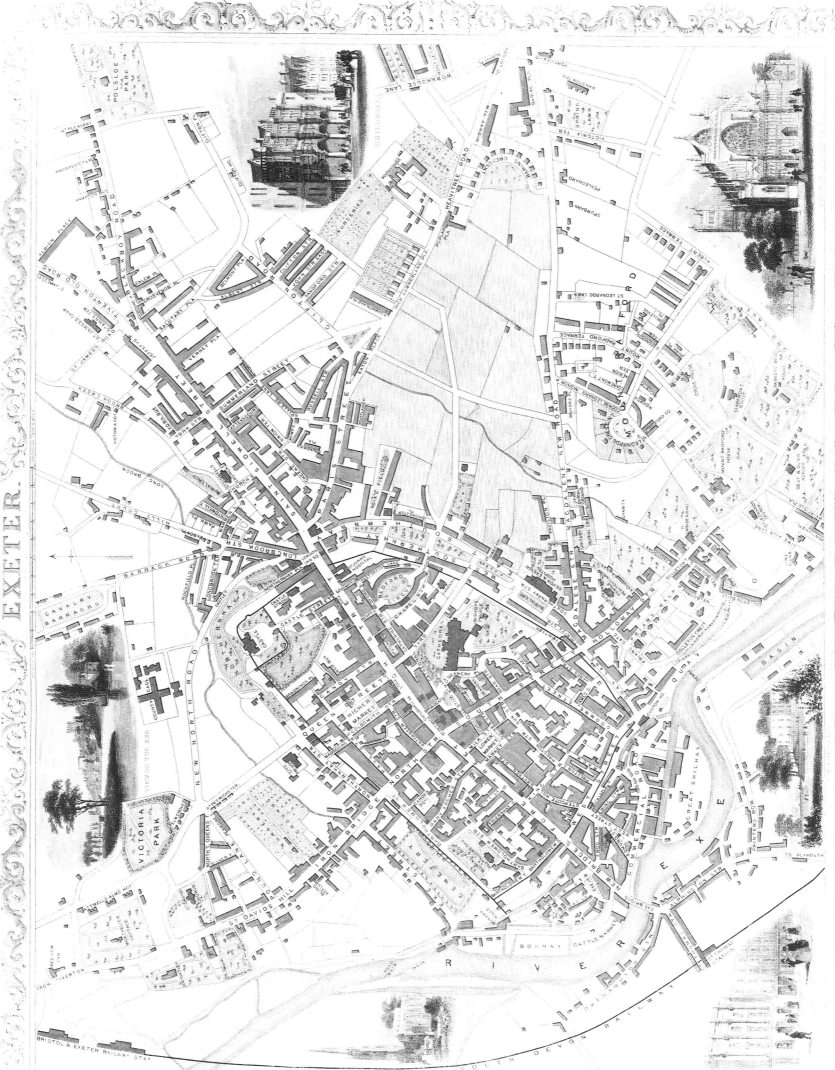

EXETER.

Glasgow

Glasgow is 43 miles from Edinburgh, and has a population of 346,984. It is a large and important city, which may be considered the metropolis and grand emporium of the west of Scotland. It is situated on the north bank of the River Clyde, here navigable, and affording the advantage of maritime communication for the purposes of commerce.

The general plan of the city is regular, the principal streets meeting in the centre, and the houses have a noble and elegant appearance. The main street, under different appellations, extends from east to west through the entire length of the city. Eastward of the cross it is named the Gallowgate; and westward, the Trongate and Argyle Street. Towards the south, branches off the Salt Market; and to the north the High Street. There are also several other streets containing handsome houses; and there are three spacious and elegant squares: St Andrew's Square, St Enoch's Square and George's Square. The cathedral is a large edifice situated on an eminence, at the north end of High Street, and is reckoned the most perfect specimen of Gothic ecclesiastical architecture remaining in Scotland.

The grand ornament of Glasgow is its college, or University, an extensive and venerable edifice which owes its origin to William Turnbull, Bishop of Glasgow in 1450.

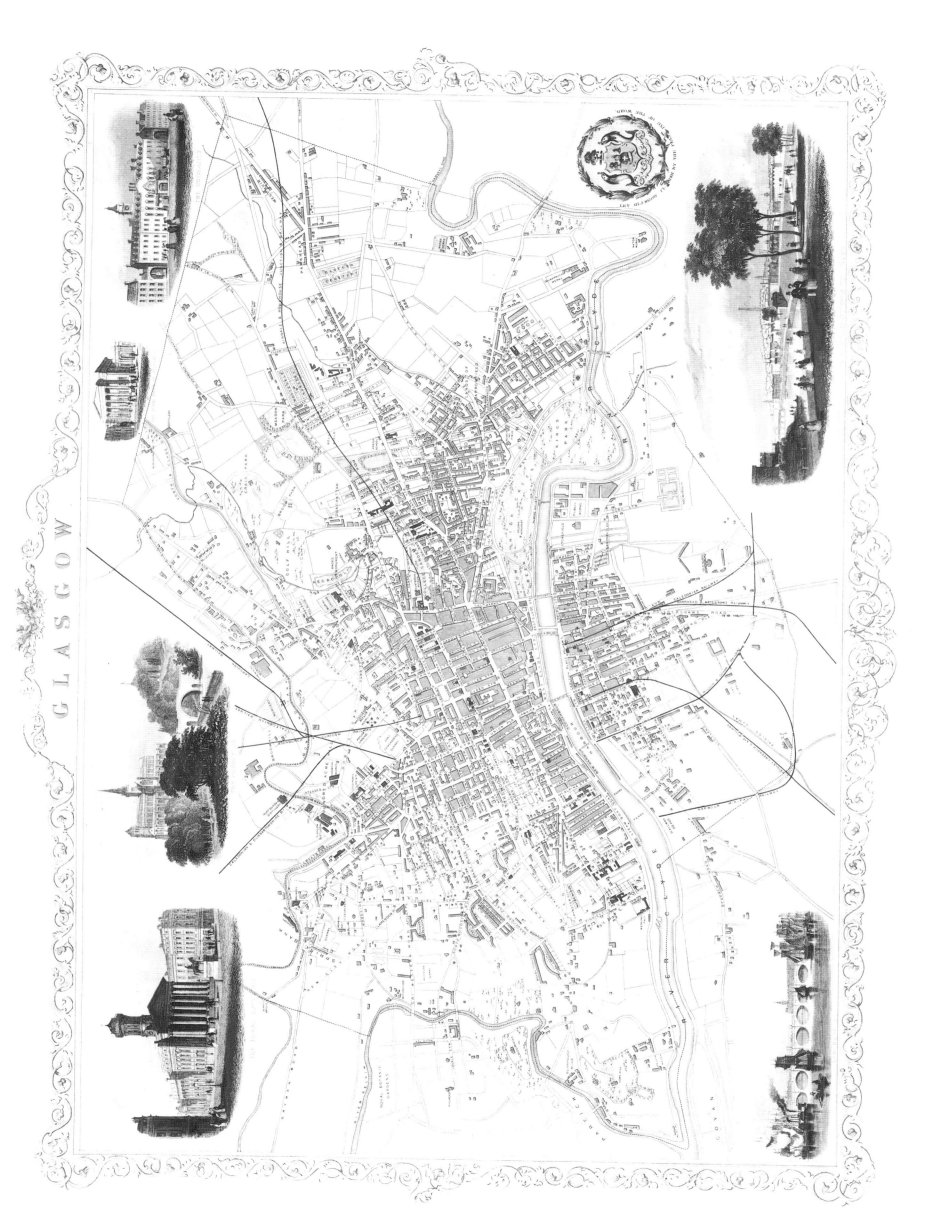

GLASGOW

JOHN TALLIS

Leeds

Leeds is 185 miles from London. The population is 273,613. It is a great town, a township, a parish, and a district in the West Riding of Yorkshire. The town stands on the River Aire, on the Leeds and Liverpool canal, at a centre of railways, 24 miles south-west of York, 42½ north-east of Manchester, and 186½ north by west of London, by railway. It is the largest town in Yorkshire, the capital of the West Riding, and the chief seat of woollen manufacture; it communicates, by inland navigation, with the eastern and western seas, and with most of the canals and navigable rivers in the kingdom; and it commands an ample system of railway conveyance in all directions, both by main lines and by connecting branches.

The general aspect of Leeds is unmistakably that of a great, rich, energetic seat of trade. Its blaze of industry, its huge factories, its splendid warehouses, its superb public buildings, instantly strike the eye of every intelligent traveller. Yet, when entered from the south or from the east, or when seen in detail, much of it looks far from handsome or pleasant. The part north of the river, or Leeds proper, was officially reported, in 1839, to contain 586 streets, of which only 244 were in good sanitary condition, while 109 were middling, 137 bad, and 96 very bad; and the part south of the river had probably a less proportional extent of good streets. Great improvements, indeed, have been made since that time – at a cost to the Corporation of not less than about £170,000 or upwards, from 1849 till 1866; and these, besides including better sewerage and higher cleanliness, have considerably altered the aggregate character and appearance of the houses.

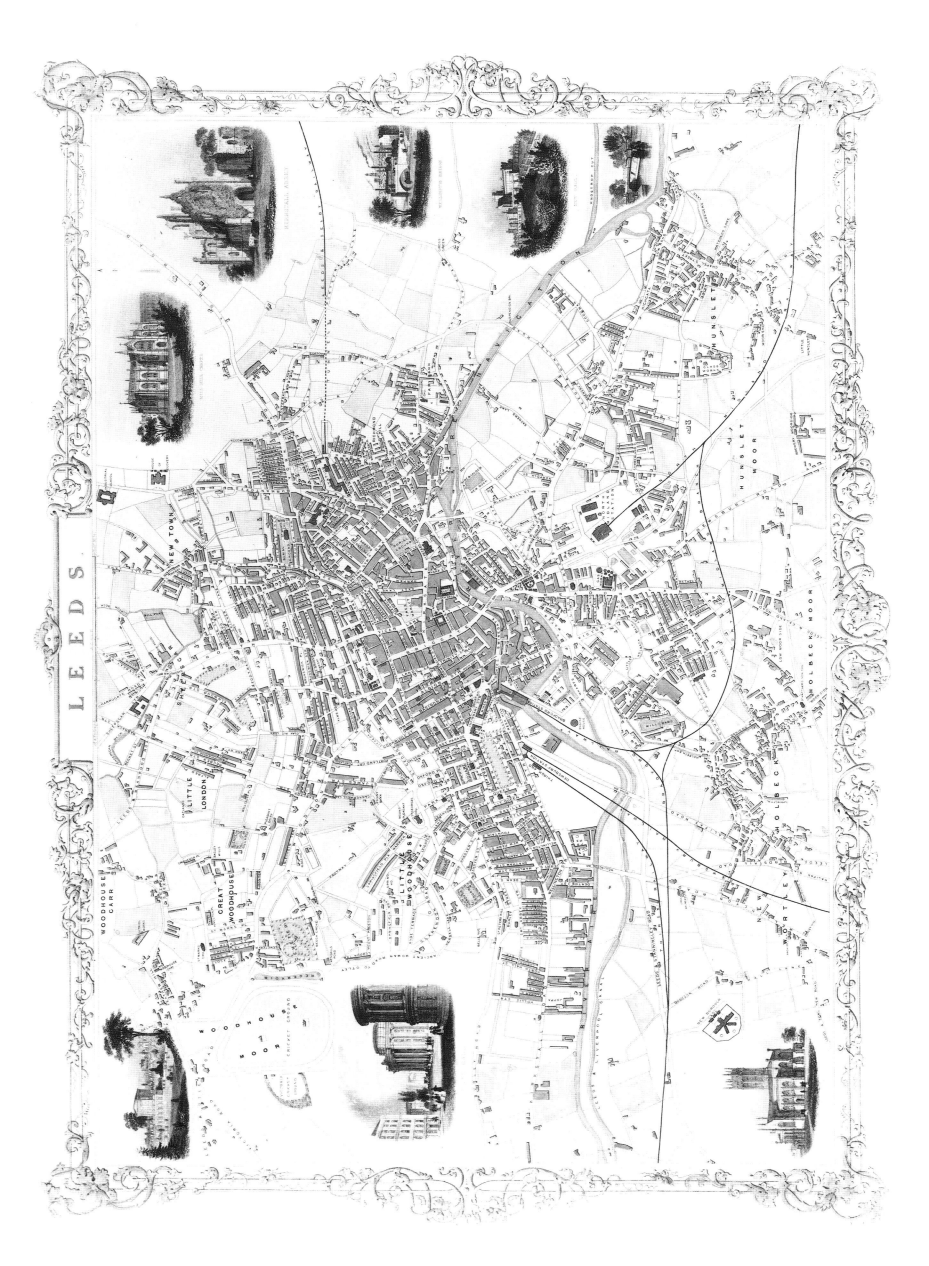

LEEDS

JOHN TALLIS

Manchester and its environs

Manchester is 189 miles from London; its population is 316,213. The city stands partly on a plain, and partly in the valley of the Irwell. The extensive circumjacent tract as seen from the nearest range of hills looks not a little charming, but does so, not from its proper character as a landscape but from its profusion of groves, villas, mansions, factories, and towns, with Manchester in the centre, and Stockport, Ashton, Oldham, Bolton, Bury, and Middleton in the distances. A stranger approaching the city, by road or by railway, bids farewell to the amenities of open scenery, makes speedy acquaintance with the smoke and noise of factories, sees the very sky changing from a clear to a greyish blue, becomes surrounded with crowded indications of traffic and manufacture, and passes at last into what seems almost a chaos of mills and warehouses.

Great improvements have for many years been in progress in the city. Outskirts which were straggling, unsightly, or rural, are now covered with ornamental suburbs. The very field of the great disastrous public meeting of 1819 is now graced with one of the chief and most ornate of the public buildings. Market Street was, so late as about 1827, a mere disagreeable lane, only wide enough to admit one ordinary sized vehicle, but is now for spaciousness and splendour, the first street in the city.

The town hall was erected in 1824, at a cost of nearly £40,000. It is in the Ionic style, copied from the temple of Erectheus at Athens and is surmounted by a dome copied from the octagonal tower of Adronicus or the Tower of the Winds.

The railway stations are Victoria Station, at Hunts Bank, for the western and northern lines of the North Western Railway; London Road Station for the southern lines of the North Western; Oxford Road Station; and New Bailey Street Station in Salford. Cotton manufacture, as of old, is still the staple manufacture of industry. The increase of it since the latter part of the last century has been stupendous. The quantity of cotton imported, about the end of last century did not exceed two million lbs per year; while the quantity imported in 1860 amounted to 1,390,938,752 lbs. The factories of various kinds in the city in 1857 comprised 96 cotton mills, 10 silk mills, 6 calico printing works, 35 dye works, 1 worsted mill, 11 hat manufactories, 16 smallware manufactories, 61 machine making establishments, 55 foundries, 4 leadworks, 4 paper-mills, 52 saw-mills, 12 corn-mills, and 1,214 miscellaneous establishments; they produced goods for storage in 1,743 warehouses.

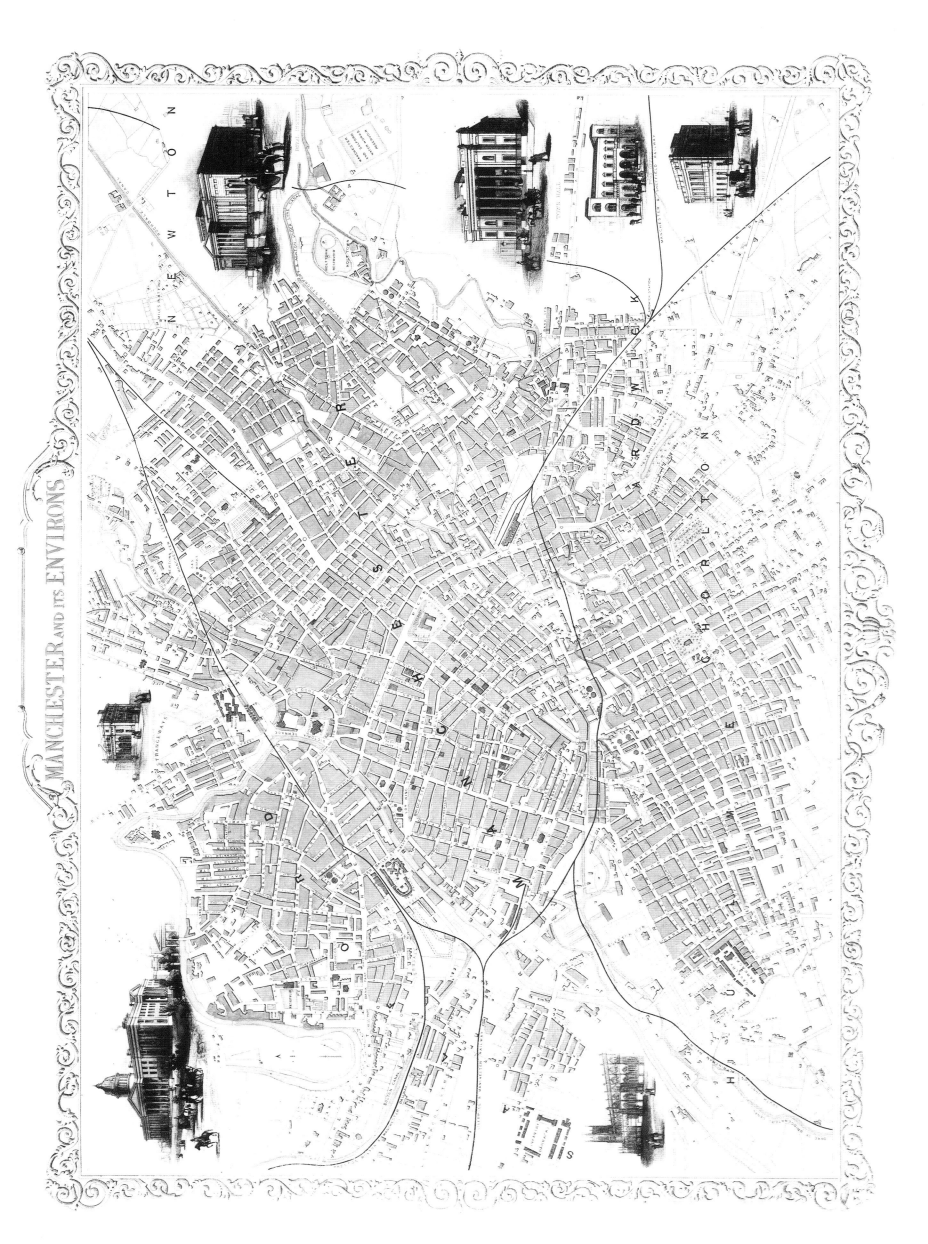

MANCHESTER AND ITS ENVIRONS

JOHN TALLIS

Newcastle upon Tyne

The population is 87,784; the city is 273 miles from London. Newcastle upon Tyne, a town in Northumberland, stands on the River Tyne at the boundary with Durham, at a focus of the north-eastern railway system, in the centre of a great coal-field, 10 miles above the influx of the Tyne to the sea. It is separated only by the Tyne from Gateshead, and has, for all business purposes, the same connexion with that town which London city has with Southwark; it is surrounded by a country which, within a radius of only a few miles, contains a population about equal to that of both itself and Gateshead.

A very narrow belt of plain along the margin of the Tyne, steep faces of three considerable eminences rising from the plain; prolonged summits of the eminences and waving hollows form the site of Newcastle. The environs are diversified, and were naturally picturesque, but have, to some extent, been defaced by manufactories and smoke. The town, till a comparatively recent period, presented a rustic appearance, amid a splendid country. So much as about one-third of even the area within the walls, as late as 1772, was disposed in lawns and gardens.

The architectural aspect of the town has very greatly changed. The old thoroughfares, even despite the large reservation of space for lawns and gardens, were aligned with a most niggardly regard to the saving of ground; they were, for the most part, mere lanes or alleys, narrow, winding, and unwholesome; and though both curtailed by inroads upon them and much improved by various kinds of alterations, they now present a striking contrast to the spacious, straight, well-built streets of the modern extensions. The old houses, also, were constructed chiefly of timber, with brick in the interstices between the beams, or covered with lath and plaster. Many of these houses still exist, and are very picturesque; but when such as they formed the entire town, they made it dismally dense and unhealthy. Even the houses of the earlier extensions were, at best, built of brick; nor were stonehouses, or at least houses of polished stone, begun until 1823.

Mr Richard Grainger, a gentleman of such humble origin as to have been proudly styled, by his admirers, 'the charity boy', began to form schemes for extensive street improvement in 1819. The town had then, indeed, been considerably renovated and enlarged, but it still presented, on the whole, a dingy appearance. Mr Grainger obtained the common council's concurrence in his plans; and during the five years thence till 1839, he constructed nine new streets of aggregately 1 mile 289 yards in length, and built the new market, the central exchange, the new theatre, the new dispensary, the music hall, a lecture-room, 2 chapels, 2 auction-marts, the incorporated company's hall, 10 inns, 12 public houses, 40 private houses, and 325 houses with shops. The value of these buildings is about £1,000,000; the ground for them cost £145,937. Grey Street, which connects some old parts of the town with a series of splendid new streets, was skilfully and tastefully subordinated to a property even higher than harmony; and is so very elegantly edificed as to be the most imposing street in the town, and one of the handsome anywhere in the empire.

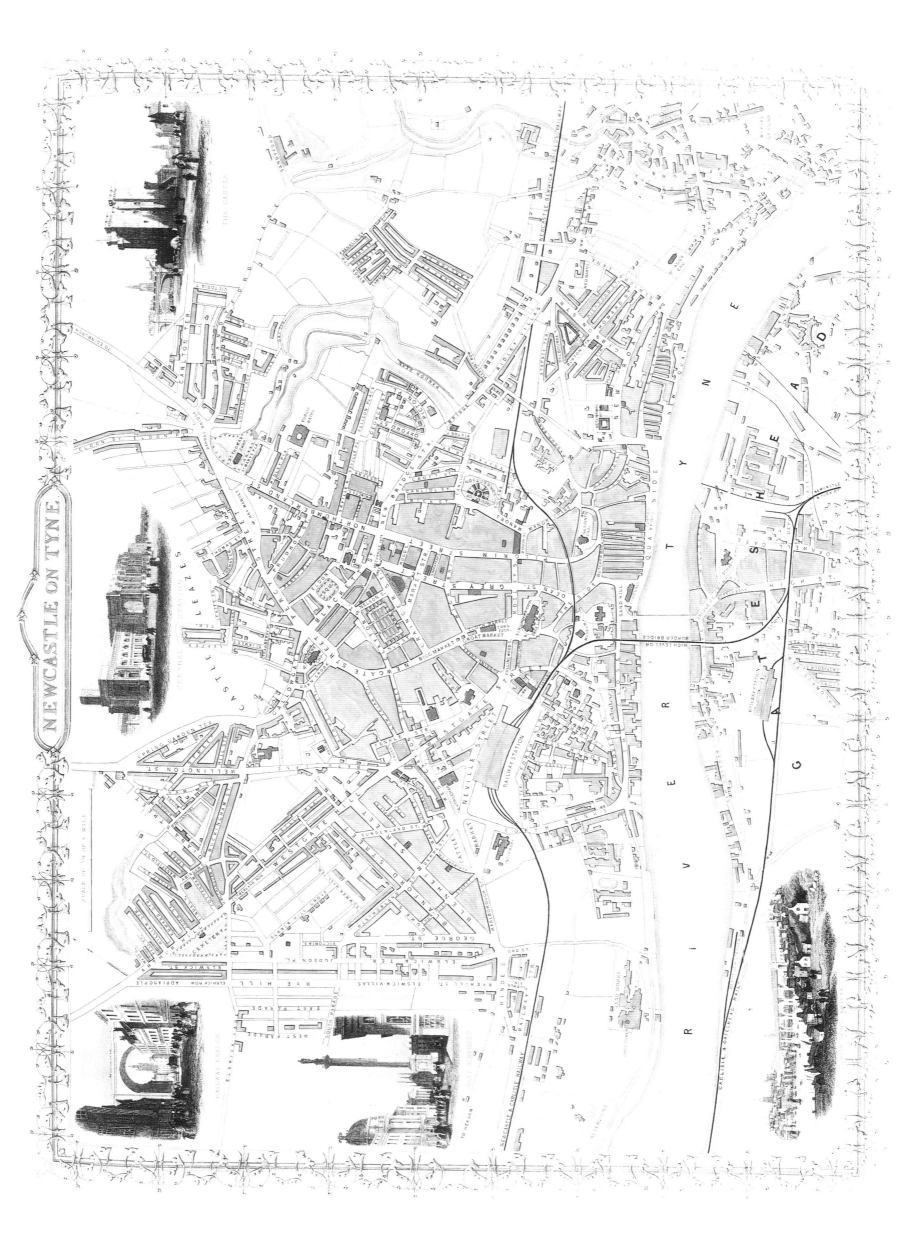

NEWCASTLE ON TYNE.

Perth

Perth is 40 miles from Edinburgh, and has a population of 22,232. It is situated on the south side of the River Tay, in the middle of an extensive plain, which it divides into two parts, called the North and South Inchs. The plan and arrangement of the streets of this town display great regularity. There are four principal streets extending from east to west, namely Mill Street, High Street, South Street and Canal Street, and these are crossed by others at right angles, forming the old part of the town.

From the foot of the High Street, a street extends in a northerly direction, called George Street, which leads to the bridge, Charlotte Street, and the New Town. There was formerly a wooden bridge across the Tay, which has been replaced by a noble stone bridge of ten arches, from the designs of Mr John Smeaton.

There is a salmon fishery on the Tay, of considerable extent, the fruits of which, either pickled or packed in ice, are sent to London. The principal manufacture here is of cotton, while manufactures of leather, shoes, boots, and gloves, are prosecuted extensively.

Printing at one time contributed considerably to the commerce of the town, and from the Perth Press proceeded an Encyclopaedia, editions of the Scottish Poets, and other works of reputation.

PERTH

NORTH INCH

RACE COURSE

RIVER TAY

ATHOLL STREET

BARRACKS

CLAY HOLES

INFIRMARY

KINNOULL CAUSEWAY

YORK PLA. COUNTY PLACE

SOUTH STREET

HIGH STREET

BARROSSA PLACE

STORMONT STR
BAROSSA STR
ROSE TERRACE

CRESCENT
ATHOLL PLACE
BLACKFRIARS
BLACKFRIARS

CHARLOTTE S

CHARLOTTE STREET

GEORGE STREET

MILL STREET

MURRAY STR

FOUNDRY LANE

UNION STR
WILLIAM STR
KINNOULL STR
BLACK

ST JOHNS PLA
ST KIRKSIDE
ST JOHNS STREET

WATERGATE

SPEYGATE

COUNTY BUILDINGS

KINNOULL
CHURCHYARD

BRIDGE

BRUCE

TO BLAIRGOWRIE
TO CUPAR

BRIDGE END

COMMERCIAL STR

TO DUNDEE

CANAL STREET

VICTORIA STREET

KING STREET
JAMES STREET
SCOTT STREET
NELSON STR
PRINCES STREET

SOUTH WILLIAM STREET

CHARLES STR

ACRES

GREYFRIARS
BURYING
GROUND

COAL
SHORE

DUNDEE & PERTH STATE

WATER
RESERVOIR

RAILWAY BRIDGE

WATER
FILTER

KINGS PLA. MARSHALL PLACE

JOINT RAILWAY TERMINUS

DUNDEE & PERTH RAILWAY

ST LEONARDS BANK

CARRS CROFT

SCOTTISH CENTRAL & NORTHERN RAILWAY

CRAIGIE BURN

ROAD TO CRAIGIE HILL

CRAIGIE

FROM EDINBURGH
ROAD TO MONCRIEFF HILL

SOUTH INCH

LIME
SHORE

MONCRIEFF ISLAND

WILLOW GATE

RIVER TAY

SCOTTISH MIDLAND RAILWAY

FROM GLASGOW

EARLS DYKE

LEONARD CAUSEWAY

PUMARTIN

JOHN TALLIS

Plymouth, Devonport and Stonehouse

The population of Plymouth is 52,221; the town lies 216 miles from London. This great seaport in the south-western extremity of Devon, comprehends the three towns of Plymouth-proper on the east, Stonehouse in the middle, and Devonport in the west, and the suburb of Morice-town on the north-west. It lies around the meeting of the South Devon and the Cornwall railway, 3½ miles from the junction of the South Devon and Tavistock railway, and 43½ miles by road, but 52¾ by railway, south-west of Exeter.

The town occupies an area of only about a mile each way; and though so comparatively limited, is not quite compact. Its site ascends boldly and brokenly from Mill-bay, Sutton-pool, and the intermediate headland; and is such as to render some of the street lines steep, and the entrance from the North-east inconvenient. Most of the streets are narrow, short, and irregular, but there is a good main thoroughfare of several names through the central parts. Multitudes of renovations have been made in the old parts, and a profusion of handsome private houses have been erected in the suburbs. Many a pleasant spot, once open for promenading has been covered with private buildings and government works; but one magnificent promenade, called the Hoe, one of the most beautiful promenades in the kingdom, remains untouched. This high ridge, extending from Mill-bay to the entrance of Sutton-pool, constitutes the sea-front of the town and commands a view, both near and far, unrivalled for variety and sparkling with all sorts of beauty.

Plymouth Sound is the outer or conjoint estuary of the Ply and the Tamar. It is famous at once as a magnificent roadstead, as a station of the British navy, and as one of the most beautiful sheets of water on the English coast. It covers about 4,500 acres, has a depth from 5 to 12 fathoms, and can accommodate 2,000 ships.

Much trade accrues from the sound being a station of the British navy; considerable trade accrues also from fisheries; and much stir occurs in spring, from extensive debarkation of emigrants to America, the Cape of Good Hope, Australia, and other parts of the World.

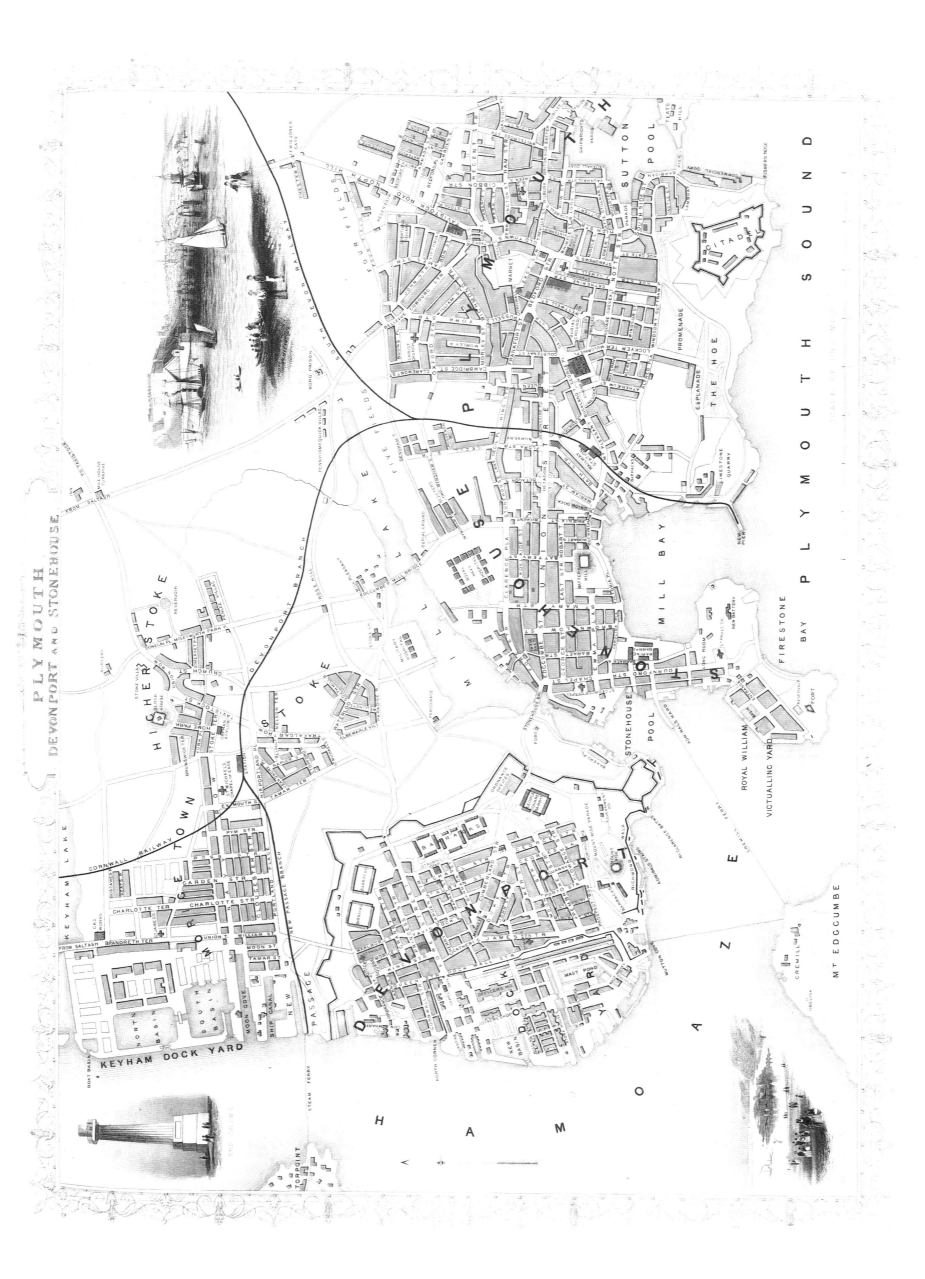

PLYMOUTH
DEVONPORT AND STONEHOUSE

PLYMOUTH SOUND

PLYMOUTH BAY

MOUTH POOL

SUTTON POOL

THE HOE

CITADEL

FIRESTONE BAY

MILL BAY

ROYAL WILLIAM VICTUALLING YARD

STONEHOUSE POOL

HAMOAZE

KEYHAM DOCK YARD

DEVONPORT DOCK YARD

MORICE TOWN

HIGHER STOKE

STOKE

TORPOINT

Mt EDGCUMBE

Preston

Preston is 217 miles from London; its population is 50,332. It is a town in Lancashire and stands on a tabular eminence, adjacent to the south end of the Lancaster canal and to the north bank of the River Ribble, at a convergence of railways, so situated with reference to the Ribble's navigation, as to be a headport; and has railway communication with all parts of the kingdom, by lines diverging at or near it towards Lancaster, Fleetwood, Liverpool, Warrington, Manchester, Blackburn, and Longridge.

The town is well built and declines gently on all sides from the centre, is well supplied with water, presents a clean and healthy appearance, and enjoys pleasant environs, with many beautiful walks and some good scenery.

The corn exchange and market-house stands on the west side of Lune Street, was erected in 1822–4, at a cost of £11,000; St. John's Church stands in Church Street, and was rebuilt in 1853–4, in the decorated English style. The public baths and wash-houses stand in Saul Street, erected in 1851, at a cost of £11,000, and are well arranged and commodious.

Markets are held on Wednesdays and Saturdays; a fair for horses begins on the Monday before the Saturday after Epiphany, and continues a week; and fairs for cattle and earthenware are held on March 27th, August 25th, and November 7th. A cotton trade struck root early, grew rapidly and is now carried on in 72 factories.

Sheffield

Sheffield is 162 miles from London, and has a population of 135,310. This town in the West Riding of Yorkshire stands at the influx of the river Sheaf to the Don, near the confluence of the Porter, the Rivelin, the Loxeley and other streams, and at a convergence of railways from Leeds, Doncaster, Worksop, Chesterfield, and Huddersfield respectively. The River Don, with the aid of a canal 4 miles long formed in 1819, gives it a navigable communication with the general canal-system of the kingdom, and with the river system of the Trent and Humber, and the railways, with their numerous ramifications and connexions, give it all the advantages of a great railway centre for all England.

The town acquired increasing skill in ironwork and cutlery, through means of artisan settlers from the Netherlands in the time of Queen Elizabeth, and began then to be famous for the manufactures of shears, sickles, knives, and scissors; and became in 1758 the mart for silver-plated goods. It therefore rose rapidly in importance; it has nearly quadrupled its population since the commencement of the present century.

The town itself stands on unequal grounds, partly eminence, partly valley, and has the advantage of being swept clean by every considerable shower. Some of the old streets are small, narrow, and irregularly built; some of even the new streets are disfigured by forges, furnaces, and other ungainly buildings; spacious squares or other large open edificed areas are totally a-wanting; and the dwelling-houses of the merchants are almost all in the outskirts or in the country, so that the town, as a whole, especially with its clouds of smoke, cannot be called attractive. Yet it has good shops, good public buildings, and some very fine suburbs. The town is well paved, well drained, and well supplied with water, has undergone much recent improvement in its street-architecture, and possesses some imposing semi-public edifices.

SHEFFIELD.

Southampton

Southampton's population is 35,305; it is 79 miles from London. This town in Hampshire stands on the River Itchin, Southampton Water, and the Southwestern railway, 12 miles from Winchester. It ranks as a great head sea-port, commands inland navigation, up the Itchin to Winchester, is a focus of railway lines for the south parts of Hampshire, and has facile railway communication with all parts of the kingdom.

Southampton fell greatly into decay after a terrible visitation of plague in 1695, experienced increase of decay from the successful rivalry of Portsmouth. The town began to revive about the beginning of the present century, through visits of the Duke of York, and through business arising from the Continental Wars, received a powerful rise from the opening of the Southwestern railway to it in 1840, and from the subsequent formation of docks. Its population increased fully six-fold between 1801 and 1861.

General markets are held on Tuesdays, Thursdays, and Saturdays; a corn-market, on Fridays; fairs, on May 6 and 7, and on Trinity Monday and Tuesday; and a regatta in August. Ship-building, coach-building, sugar-refining, brewing, and the manufacture of silks and carpets are carried on.

Commerce is much more extensive than trade. The harbour is both capacious and facile, and has excellent artificial appurtenances. A wooden landing-pier, 1,000 feet long and 36 feet wide, was constructed in 1833, at a cost of £30,000. A tidal dock of 16 acres, with 3,100 feet of quayage, and with from 18 to 21 feet of water, was completed in 1842, at a cost of £140,000. There are also a floating dock for ships, a dock for colliers, and three graving docks. The vessels belonging to the port, at the beginning of 1844, were 136 small sailing vessels, of aggregately 3,713 tons, 110 large sailing vessels, of aggregately 15,106 tons; 14 small vessels of aggregately 404 tons, and 24 large steam vessels, of aggregately 7,651 tons.

SOUTHAMPTON

THE BAR GATE

THE PARK

RESERVOIR

RESERVOIR

PORTSWOOD

HIGHFIELD HO.

PORTSWOOD LODGE

CHRIST CH.

HIGHFIELD LANE

SCHOOL

ST DENNIS PRIORY

WESTWOOD HO. PARK

BEVOIS MOUNT

BANNISTER LODGE

SOUTH WESTERN RAILWAY

BITTERNE ROAD

ARCHER'S LODGE

BEVOIS VALLEY

BEDFORD PLACE

SPRING HILL HO.

BELLE VUE

BEREKLEY ROAD

NORTHAM

SHIP YARD

IRON WORKS

TIMBER PONDS

MILLSTONE POINT

BOAT HARBOUR

PRINCES STR.

YORK STR.

CLARENCE ST.

KENT ST.

BELVIDERE

BELVIDERE ROAD

SHIP YARD

RIVER ITCHEN

ELMS

ST PETER'S CH.

CHARLOTTE PL.

EAST MAGDALENS

WEST MAGDALENS

CUMBERLAND PL.

MARKET GARDENS

ROMSEY HILL

MILLBROOK ROAD

HAMILTON COMMERCIAL ROAD

NEW ROAD

DORCHESTER RAILWAY WESTERN

STATION

FAIR FIELD

KINGS

HOUND WELL

HOGLANDS

BEVOIS ST.

JAMES STR.

CUMBERLAND

COLEMAN

ST MARYS STR.

BRITANNIA WHARF

HOE'S WHARF

UNION WHARF

BALTIC WHARF

AMERICAN WHARF

NEW DOCK

GAS WORKS

VICTORIA ROOMS

MANCHESTER

HANGER BUILD

UPPER EAST

HIGH STREET ABOVE BAR STR.

CHANTREY MEADOWS

ANGLE SEAT

PEARTREE GREEN

OLD FERRY

PUBLIC CRICKET GROUND

TIMBER PONDS

OAK BANK HO.

ITCHEN

LONG ROOM

WEST QUAY

QUEENS MEADOWS

RAILWAY TERMINUS

BRIDGE ROAD

CANUTE ROAD

FLOATING BRIDGE

TOLL H.

TIMBER PONDS

CLIFF HOTEL

WOOLSTON ROAD

WOOLSTON HOTEL

CRICKET GROUND

DOWLINGS LANE

TRAMWAY

CUSTOM HOUSE

WEST QUATE

CLOSE DOCK

TIDAL DOCK

NETLEY ABBEY.

SOUTHAMPTON

York

York is 199 miles from London; its population is 28,842. This city in Yorkshire stands on Watling Street, on the River Ouse at the influx of the Foss, and at a divergence of railways in five directions. It was a centre of Roman roads, coming to it in five directions; it is now a centre of railway communication, from London to Edinburgh, and from coast to coast; it commands sea-ward navigation by the Ouse, and very extensive inland navigation through the Ouse's connections.

The city's structure, till about the commencement of the present century, was remarkably antique and singular; and, notwithstanding numerous and sweeping changes which have been made upon it, still presents a striking mixture of ancient features with modern ones.

A general weekly market is held on Saturday, a cattle market on alternate Tuesdays; a wool market on every Thursday from Lady-day to Michaelmas; a leather market on the first Wednesday of March, June, September and December; fairs on Whit-Monday, July 10th, August 12th, and November 23rd; and a horse show, during the entire week before Christmas.

Commerce has never been so extensive as the facilities for export might have made it, and is now less than formerly. A considerable trade is done in drugs, tea, coffee, and confectionery. The general retail trade is very large. The manufacture of linens was at one time flourishing, but fell away. The making of combs, gloves, shoes, saddlery, and glass is considerable, and there are roperies, tanneries, breweries, and large foundries.

The police force, in 1864, comprised 40 men, at an annual cost of £2,592. The crimes committed, in 1863, were 82; the persons apprehended, 78.

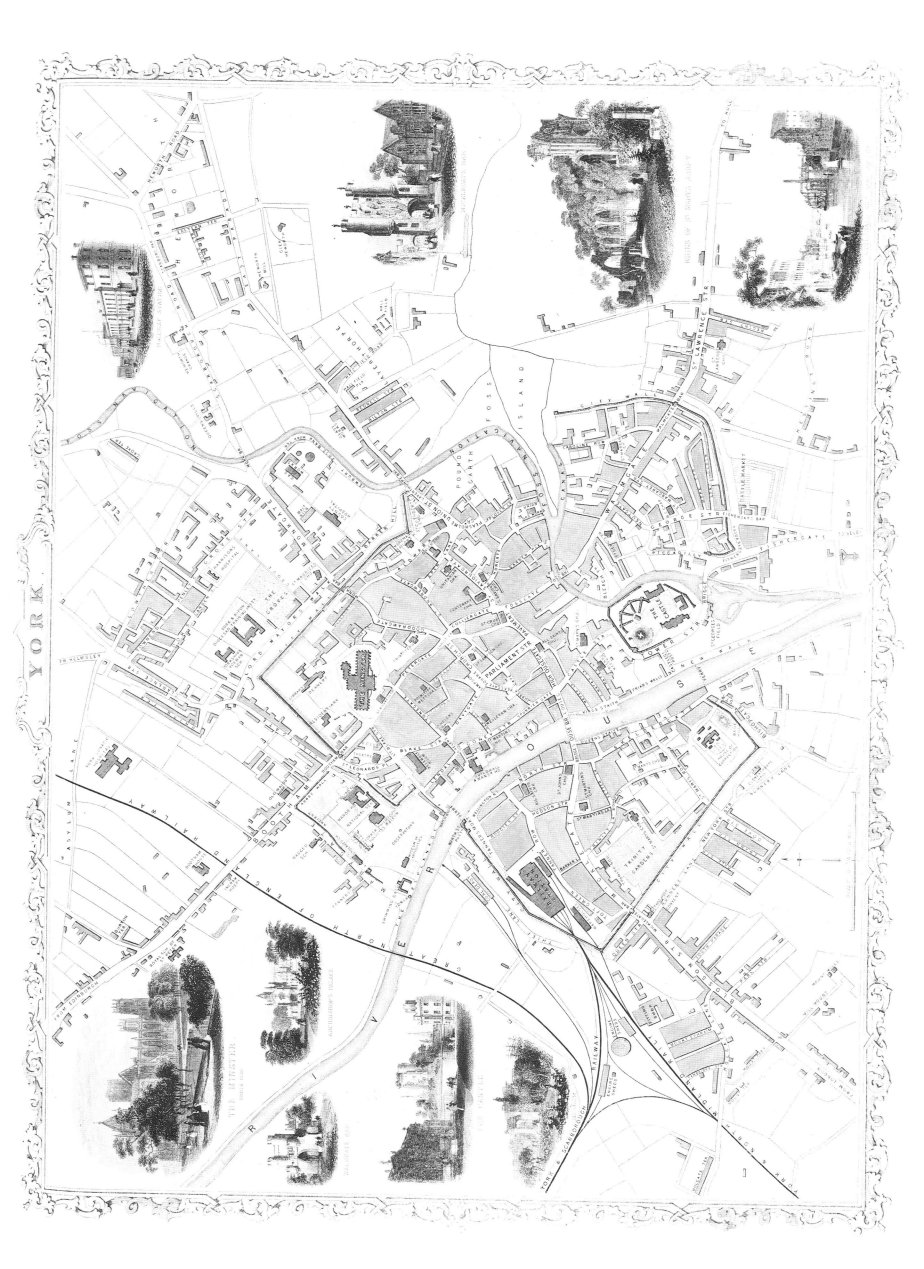

YORK.

RUINS OF ST MARY'S ABBEY

THE MINSTER SOUTH SIDE

Bibliography

Barclay, James, *Barclay's Complete and Universal Dictionary*, London, 1842.

Britton, John and Brayley, Edward, *The Beauties of England and Wales*, London, 1801–1818.

Gorton, John, *Topographical Dictionary of Great Britain and Ireland*, London, 1831–1833.

Lewis, Samuel, *Topographical Dictionary of England*, London, 1831.

Lewis, Samuel, *Topographical Dictionary of Ireland*, London, 1837.

Lewis, Samuel, *Topographical Dictionary of Scotland*, London, 1837.

Smith, David, *Victorian Maps of the British Isles*, London, 1985.

Tallis, John, *Tallis's Topographical Dictionary of England and Wales*, London, c 1860.

Wilson, John Marius, *The Imperial Gazeteer of England and Wales*, London, 1866–1869.

Acknowledgements and Picture Credits

*The publishers would like to thank the following for their kind
co-operation and permission to reproduce maps from their
collections:*

The Royal Geographical Society, London

Jonathan Potter Ltd, 21 Grosvenor Street, London

The author, Ashley Baynton-Williams

O'Shea Gallery, 89 Lower Sloane Street, London

Tooley, Adams & Co, 13 Cecil Court, London

Special thanks also to Derek Allen for all his help on this book.